THE

ABSOLUTE

BASICS

OF THE

CHRISTIAN

FAITH

THE ABSOLUTE
BASICS OF THE
CHRISTIAN
FAITH

PHIL TALLON

Seedbed

Scripture quotations are taken from THE HOLY BIBLE, NEW INTERNATIONAL VERSION®, NIV® Copyright © 1973, 1978, 1984, 2011 by Biblica, Inc.™ Used by permission. All rights reserved worldwide.

Printed in the United States of America

Paperback ISBN: 978-1-62824-297-3
uPDF ISBN: 978-1-62824-298-0

Library of Congress Control Number: 2016941807

Cover and inside illustrations by Andrew Chandler
Cover design and page layout by Nick Perreault at Strange Last Name

SEEDBED PUBLISHING
Franklin, Tennessee
seedbed.com

To the students and ministry staff
at Christ Church
Memphis, Tennessee

Contents

Unit 6: Doctrine of the Spirit

Unit 7: Doctrine of the Church

Unit 8: Doctrine of Last Things

Preface and Acknowledgments

This book grew out of my experiences as a youth pastor. Specifically, it grew out of a need to have an introduction to key Christian beliefs that was clear, biblical, unapologetically traditional, and compelling for people with little to no background knowledge.

Though there are many introductions to Christian theology that are available, almost all of them are aimed at readers with at least some measure of theological training or interest. Teaching in the church, especially to students in their early teens, I searched far and wide for a text that assumed no background knowledge and also sparked a desire to understand the basic teachings of the church.

Finding nothing that quite fit the bill, I set out to create this book, along with videos that were fun and engaging.

This material has already been tested out in a number of churches, and the reports back indicate that the work is achieving its goal. The catechism, memory verses, text, and videos all seem to meet a need in the church for a clear, compelling introduction to Christian belief.

I cannot thank enough my fellow student ministry staff and volunteers who helped me to prepare and teach this material. I want to personally thank Fitz, Carolyn, Beth, Ty, Mary Elizabeth, and Bowman. Special thanks to Dallas, who graciously made space for me in his ministry to teach this material, and was a source of continual support during the whole process.

Many others helped to bring this project to life. They provided material that has worked its way into the book in many ways (ideas, examples, key verses, and accompanying materials). They are:

» Tom Fuerst
» Kathy & Richard Turner
» Beth Ann Cook
» Joshua Smith
» Guy Williams
» Dave Harrity
» Matthew Johnson
» Matt Dampier
» Derek King
» Brian Marshall
» C. J. Carter
» Josh Grant
» Teddy Ray
» Jonathan Powers
» Jason Jackson
» J. D. Walt & the rest of the Seedbed crew

This project would not be what it is without the assured pen and creative mind of Andrew Chandler, a skilled illustrator whose work is infused with his wit, talent, and Christian devotion in every line he drew.

Finally, this book would not exist without the unfailing support of my family, including my wife's wonderful parents who live with my wife and me, and who help us raise our four children. Special thanks to my wonderful wife, Karen, who never begrudged me time on the weekends to complete the manuscript when there were many more needful things to be done around the house.

How to Use This Book

This book has three main elements:

1. A basic *catechesis* with theological questions and answers, along with Bible verses for memorization. These lay out the most basic elements of Christian theology in plain language.

2. Sixteen *lessons* that comment on the catechesis questions and answers. The lessons explain the central ideas using clear analogies and illustrations and follow immediately after the memory verses.

3. *Notes* for those who want to dive deeper into the key ideas. (The Notes are in the back of the book.

Anyone can pick up this book and read it on their own. But it is designed so that it can be used to lead groups through the big ideas of the faith. If you are using this in a class setting, such as a new member or confirmation class in church, or as a small-group study, here are some suggestions:

The questions, answers, and Bible verses are intended to be easily memorized so that a class that is working through the material (or an individual on his own) can carry around in their heads the core teachings of the church. Memorization is never easy at first, but it gets easier with practice. Most students and adults do have the ability to memorize these questions, answers, and memory verses (even if they don't realize it). A good practice is to have all people in the class recite the questions, answers, and the memory verses at the beginning of the class.

The lessons are short, so that anyone can read through them quickly. Teachers leading students through the material should have everyone read the lessons ahead of time and begin to think through the ideas so they will be ready for discussion. There are also fun, illustrated videos of the text, which are available through Seedbed's website. When a class gathers together, I would suggest showing the videos and then breaking into groups to discuss, then gather together again to talk about the key ideas and make sure everyone understands them.

The notes (indicated by this symbol: 🧩) provide more in-depth discussion of the ideas at play. Teachers who are leading students or adults through the material should read these sections so that they have a better sense of what's going on behind the scenes: specifically how the church has worked to faithfully articulate what the Bible teaches in a way that holds everything together rationally. **There are also teachers' guides (available online at seedbed.com/absolutebasics) to provide discussion questions, activities, lesson plans, and other resources.** There are references throughout the notes to books that provide helpful additional reading. If teachers only want to pick up an additional book or two for background reading, I recommend *Thirty Questions: A Short Catechism of the Christian Faith* by Timothy Tennent, or (for a much deeper dive) *Classic Christianity: A Systematic Theology* by Thomas Oden.

THE

ABSOLUTE

BASICS

OF THE

CHRISTIAN

FAITH

Catechesis Questions and Memory Verses

Q1. Who is God?

    A. God is the Holy Trinity: Father, Son, and Holy Spirit. Three persons in one God. (2 Corinthians 13:14)

Q2. What is God like?

    A. God is perfect in power, knowledge, and in His holy love. (Psalm 147:5)

Q3. What did God make?

    A. God spoke everything into being, by His own free choice, and it was very good. (Hebrews 11:3)

Q4. Why is there evil?

    A. God gave us free will to obey and we did not. (Romans 5:12)

Q5. Who is Jesus Christ?

    A. The eternally begotten Son of God and the Son of Mary. Fully divine. Fully human. (John 1:14)

Q6. Why did the Son of God become human?

    A. Because God loves us and wants to make us true children of God. (Galatians 4:4–5)

Q7. What is salvation?

A. Through Jesus' sacrificial death and victorious resurrection, we are reconciled with God and rescued from destruction.
(1 Timothy 2:5–6)

Q8. What is required for salvation?

A. We must repent and believe in Jesus Christ. (Mark 1:15)

Q9. What are the benefits of salvation?

A. We are pardoned by God, made part of God's family again, and given resurrection life and power. (Romans 5:1)

Q10. What happens when we live out our salvation in Christ?

A. God continues to work in us to make us holy and blameless.
(Colossians 1:22)

Q11. Who is the Holy Spirit?

A. The eternal Spirit of God, who proceeds from the Father and the Son. (John 14:26)

Q12. What does the Holy Spirit do?

A. The Spirit leads us to repentance, gives us new life, and empowers us to follow Jesus. (Titus 3:5–6)

Q13. What is the church?

A. The church is the community of all true believers, who are Christ's body in the world, continuing the work of the apostles.
(Ephesians 4:4–5)

Q14. What are the church's sacraments?

A. Baptism is the holy covenant by which we join the church, and Holy Communion is the church's ongoing act of thanksgiving. Both are means of participating in Jesus' death and resurrection.
(Matthew 28:19–20)

Q15. What is the world's great hope?

    A. Christ has died. Christ has risen. Christ will come again to redeem all things and reign as King forever. (Revelation 22:20)

Q16. What is our future?

    A. Like Jesus, we will be raised from the dead, either to worship God forever or to be forever separated from Him. (1 Corinthians 6:14)

WHO IS GOD?

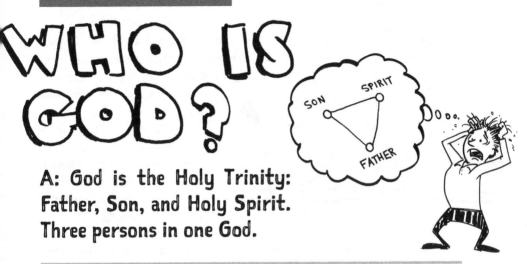

A: God is the Holy Trinity: Father, Son, and Holy Spirit. Three persons in one God.

May the grace of the Lord Jesus Christ, and the love of God, and the fellowship of the Holy Spirit be with you all. —2 Corinthians 13:14

The Trinity is one of the most important theological ideas ever. But it gives people panic attacks when they think about it. This lesson will give you the very basics you need to understand what the Trinity is, and why it matters so much.

The basic idea behind the Trinity is this: God is three things, but also still one thing. ✳

God is three persons who have existed for all eternity, are equally powerful, wise, and good, and who have always depended on each other.

THE **3** PERSONS of the TRINITY HAVE ALWAYS EXISTED

There's the Father, the Son, and the Spirit, existing in perfect harmony as one God.

How can this be? How can you have three things that exist perfectly together?

(7)

Here's the thing, if you can understand a tiny bit about how music works, you can understand the basics of the Trinity.

Find a piano. Pick any white key, put your thumb on it. Then skip a white key and put your index finger on the next one. Then skip one more and put your middle finger on the next white key. Now press down your thumb, then index finger, then middle finger. Boom. There's a harmonic chord. Three distinct sounds all existing in a perfect harmony.

Three things that are also one thing. The threeness and the oneness work together perfectly.

This gives us a picture (or rather a sound) of what God is like. There is one God (like the one chord) with three persons (like the three notes) all existing in perfect harmony forever.

Now, unlike the chord we just played, which came into being then ceased to exist, the three persons of the Trinity have always existed. And they've always existed in the relationship of Father, Son, and Holy Spirit.

The Father has always been the Father of the Son. (You can't be a father without a son.) The Son has always been Son to the Father. And they have always been unified by the love of the Spirit.

What this means is that the most basic fact about all reality is loving relationship. Before there was a world, there was a family: the family of the triune God.

So when you get down to the very bottom of things—to the root of all reality— there's love.

C. S. Lewis makes this interesting point in *Mere Christianity*,

> All sorts of people are fond of repeating the Christian statement that "God is love." But, they seem not to notice that the words "God is love" have no real meaning unless God contains at least two Persons. Love is something that one person has for another person. If God was a single person, then before the world was made, He was not love. 4

The fact that God is perfectly loving requires that God is relational. And the opposite is true as well. The fact that God is relational requires that God is perfectly loving. Here's why. If God is triune we know that God is love, because you can't have three people existing for all eternity in harmonious relationship if they aren't perfectly loving.

Imagine existing for all eternity with your brothers and sisters, or even your friends. Eventually you would get in some fights. But the Father, Son, and Holy Spirit don't fight. Because God is perfectly loving.

We know God is love because God is a *Trinity.*

We know God is a Trinity because God is *love.*

So the Trinity is this perfect, loving relationship that's always existed. One God in three persons.

And because the Trinity is one God, the persons work together in everything they do.

In Matthew 28:19, Jesus said we are baptized in the name of the Father, Son, and Holy Spirit. The entire Trinity is at work in saving us, so we must name the whole Trinity as we're made part of Christ's body through baptism. 5

And it's not just baptism, all throughout the story of Jesus we see all three persons at work. There's a pattern here.

The Father is the source of everything and He sends the Son into the world in the power of the Spirit.

» We see this in Jesus' birth. By the Holy Spirit, the Son of God is born into the world (Luke 1:35).
» We see this in Jesus' baptism. The Son carries out the mission of the Father in the power of the Spirit (Luke 3:21–23).
» We see this in Jesus' blessing of His disciples when He ascends. When the Son goes back to the Father He sends the Spirit to empower us (John 15:26).

Did you detect the pattern? Here it is again.

The Father is the source and goal of our salvation. Jesus is the way. And the Holy Spirit is the power to get there. 🌑

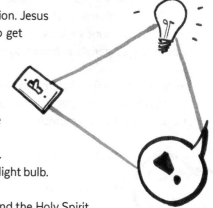

Imagine it like this:

» The Father is the one who says, "Let there be light."
» The Son goes and flips on the light switch.
» The Spirit is the electricity that powers the light bulb.

The Father is the source. The Son is the way. And the Holy Spirit is the power.

Another way of thinking about this is to imagine yourself kneeling to pray the Lord's Prayer. We are praying the prayer Jesus taught us. Now imagine Jesus is standing beside you. We begin by praying, "Our Father." Jesus is helping us to have right relationship with the Father. Now imagine that it's the Holy Spirit inside you who is giving you the power to pray the prayer Jesus taught us.

The Son beside you. The Father above you. The Spirit inside you. All working to give us a right relationship with God.

The Father is the source. The Son is the way. And the Holy Spirit is the power.

All this might seem a bit mysterious and complicated. But the nice thing is that once you start looking for the Trinity, you see it everywhere. For instance, the very words of the Apostle's Creed are shaped by the Trinity. We begin with the Father (the source), move to the Son (the way), and end with the Spirit and the Spirit's area of work (empowering the church). ✹

The Father above you. Jesus beside you. The Spirit inside you. There you go. There's the Trinity.

WHAT IS GOD LIKE?

A: God is perfect in power, knowledge, and in His holy love.

Great is our Lord and mighty in power; his understanding has no limit. —Psalm 147:5

As we've just discussed, God is three persons: Father, Son, and Holy Spirit.

Three persons in one God. They are distinct in their personhood but united in their nature. Nature is maybe a bit of a hard word, so let me explain. Nature here means the "kind of thing" something is.

> » Ice cream's nature is to be a frozen milk product.
> » A giraffe's nature is to be a long-necked, even-toed ungulate mammal.
> » A triangle's nature is to be a closed figure with three sides and three angles.

So what's God's nature? What kind of thing is God?

The best way to speak about God's nature is to say that God is, in every way, a perfect kind of thing. God's nature is whatever is best.

Saint Anselm, a medieval monk, described God as "supremely great." God is so great, for Anselm, that He's the greatest being we can imagine. It's impossible to even think of a being greater than God. If we could think of something truly better than our definition of God, then we should change our definition so that God would be understood as that better thing.

This is what we mean when we say that God is "a perfect being." We can't think of anything better.

The idea of perfection is important because we are called not only to love God, but also to worship Him. Worship means to offer total devotion. And only a perfect being is truly worthy of worship. Though the Bible teaches that angels surpass us in power, we do not worship them.

Worshiping anything less than a perfect being is sinful. The Bible has a word for worshiping less-than-perfect things. It's called idolatry. This is why the psalmist said, "For all the gods of the nations are idols, but the LORD made the heavens" (Ps. 96:5).

The true God can't be a lesser deity with some powers. Zeus, for instance, from Greek mythology, had a lot of power. He could throw lightning bolts. But he didn't create lightning. Zeus wasn't even eternal. According to the mythological stories, Zeus had a father and came into being at a particular point in time.

The only God worthy of worship is perfectly powerful, wise, good, eternal, and is the Creator of anything that exists.

One of the ways that we know from Scripture that Jesus is the true God is that He is worshiped. After His resurrection, when Jesus met the women at the tomb, the Bible says that the women "came to him, clasped his feet and worshiped him" (Matt. 28:9). Jesus is worthy of worship because He is the true God—the second person of the Trinity. And God is perfect.

Now, in order to understand perfection, we have a little bit of a problem. True perfection is hard to describe, because *we're* not perfect. Imperfect people have a hard time knowing exactly what a perfect being would be like. It's like trying to imagine how a person *smarter than you* would think.

So immediately we're in trouble.

It's a little bit like this. We can think of the idea of a perfect circle but when we try to draw one it's very hard. We mess up. Likewise, we can imagine the idea of a perfect God even if we can't actually describe all the things this perfect God would be like.

Fortunately the Bible helps us out by telling us some things about God's perfection. Scripture tells us, among other things, that God's perfection means that God is perfectly powerful (Luke 1:37), perfectly knowing (Matthew 6:8), and perfectly good (Matthew 5:48).

This means:

> » God *can do anything.*
> » God *knows everything.*
> » God *will always do what is right.*

For us, this is really good news, because this means that we can fully trust God. He knows us completely and loves us perfectly. Nothing (except for us) can stop God from achieving the good plans He has for us.

If God wasn't perfect in this way, we might not be able to fully trust Him.

If God had all the power, but wasn't perfectly wise, He could be kind of destructive.

If God was perfectly smart, but wasn't perfectly good, He might be kind of a villain.

If God was perfectly good, but didn't know us or have the power to save us, He would be kind of useless.

Take this example. Imagine you have three super-heroes: *Power Person*, *Genius Guy*, and *Moral Man*.

» *Power Person* can do anything, but he's not very smart. So whenever he tries to help, he often does the wrong thing.

» *Genius Guy* knows everything, but he isn't fully good. So sometimes he helps, but sometimes he uses his brilliance for his own selfish ends.

» *Moral Man* knows exactly what the right thing is to do, and he desires to do it, but he isn't all-powerful or all-knowing. So even though he wants to help everybody, he can't. He's just a guy.

If you got in trouble, which of these three would you call?

It's hard to say. None of them might be any help.

The good news is that God is Power Person, Genius Guy, and Moral Man all rolled into one. He has all the power, all the knowledge, and is perfectly good.

So we can *always* trust Him.

WHAT DID GOD MAKE?

A. God spoke everything into being, by His own free choice, and it was very good.

By faith we understand that the universe was formed at God's command, so that what is seen was not made out of what was visible. —Hebrews 11:3

In the beginning there was just God. Life was good. God had everything He needed. The Father, Son, and Holy Spirit were perfect and perfectly happy.

But God decided, of His own free choice, to do something extra. He decided to make a universe. And so, *KABOOM*, there was an eruption of creativity. God made a universe.

The Bible teaches that God made the world:

» by His will (Revelation 4:11)
» from nothing (Hebrews 11:3).

God is so powerful that He didn't need to make the universe out of anything. He created all the matter in the universe and put it in a beautiful order.

There's a joke that goes like this: Some engineers figure out how to create life out of dirt, and so they go to God and say, "We're as powerful as you now. We can make life just like you can." And God says, "Okay, let me see." So the engineers start to sweep together enough dirt to make a human, but God says, "Hold on right there. Use your *own* dirt."

Humans can make things *with* matter, but we can't *make* matter.

God not only made life out of dirt; He made the dirt too.

Not only this, but God *spoke* the universe into being (Genesis 1:3; Hebrews 11:3). All God had to do was speak and there everything was. If God says, "elephants," then there are some elephants.

The Bible tells us that this speaking, the "word" of God though which God made the world, was the work of the Son (Colossians 1:16). The life, the universe, and every-thing was brought into being by God's "Word"—which is Jesus (John 1:3).

And the Spirit was there too, giving life to everything God made through His Son. The breath that is breathed into humanity is the work of the Holy Spirit (Genesis 2:7).

So the whole Trinity—Father, Son, and Holy Spirit—teamed up to make the universe.

The Bible also says that the universe—filled with mountains, clouds, bushes, mushrooms, anemones, mountain goats, giraffes, and people—was very good.

There's a word we have for things that people make that are good and freely given. That word is "gift." The creation of life was a *gift*. God didn't have to do it. But He wanted to. And God is a very good gift-giver.

17

The natural response to a gift is thankfulness. When someone gives you something the right thing to do is give thanks. Maybe after a birthday party when you were a kid your parents handed you a stack of cards to write thank-you notes to the people who gave you the gifts.

This part of getting a gift is rarely fun but it's the right thing to do. That's why parents do it. Because it's right, and will hopefully teach us to carry the practice into our adult lives.

So if you're a kid who's being made to do it, or a well-trained adult, after getting a gift, you sit down and tell the person who gave you the present how much you appreciate them and the gift they gave.

Well, this applies in a similar way to our relationship to God. The way that we show our gratitude to God for the gift of existence is by *obedience*.

God gives us life and a world to live in, and our response is to say thanks to God by obeying Him.

Gifts often come with strings attached. And this isn't necessarily a bad thing.

Imagine on your sixteenth birthday you look outside and see a new car. It's just the one you always dreamed of. Maybe it's a Jeep, or a sports car, or a big truck. Now imagine that your parents say to you, "But first, you need to learn how to drive it." But instead of saying thanks you run out and hop in, turn the key, and drive off. But you don't know where the brake is so the first thing that happens is you get in a pile-up and wreck the car.

That would be about the most ungrateful thing you could do: taking the gift from your parents, but not bothering to obey them, or even learning how to use the gift the right way.

Well, that's a lot like what happened when God gave us the gift of life. We took the gift, but did not take the conditions that went with the gift. The result was ruin.

Genesis 1-3 paints a picture of a God who gives extravagantly. He made an entire world and placed humans in it to be His representatives. It was a world filled to overflowing with beautiful things: animals, rivers, and trees. In the story, humans were given every kind of tree to eat from (Genesis 2:9, 15). Only one single thing was forbidden: to eat from one specific tree. And that was the one we ate from.

This is like going to Disney World and being told that every ride is working and ready for us, but one ride is dangerous, and in need of repairs. And then going straight to that one dangerous ride, and forcing our way onto it.

G. K. Chesterton, a British journalist who lived at the turn of the twentieth century, wrote about the way that sometimes very good gifts still have conditions. He used the example of fairy tales to communicate this. In fairy tales, very often something wonderful, unexpected, and magical happens, but there is a rule that comes with the spell: a *requirement* that comes with the *enchantment*.

He gives the example of Cinderella. Against all odds, Cinderella is allowed to go to the ball in high style because her fairy godmother suddenly appears and does some fine magic to give her a dress, glass slippers, and a carriage. But there's a catch. Cinderella must be back by midnight.

As Chesterton points out, it would show a certain ingratitude for Cinderella to complain about the *necessity* of the rule, given how *unnecessary* was the gift.
He wrote, "If Cinderella says, 'How is it that I must leave the ball at twelve?' her godmother might answer, 'How is it that you are going there till twelve?'" ✳

If some extravagant gift comes with a small requirement, perhaps we would be better off meditating on the *unexpected pleasure* rather than the *insignificant prohibition*.

The same goes for Adam and Eve, and for us as well. Seeing the world, and life itself, as a *gift* changes everything.

Now, there's more to be said about the way the world is a gift.

Because it is not just that God has simply given us the world once. It is true that God created all things out of nothing, by His own free will. But the Bible also says that God is "sustaining all things by his powerful word" (Heb. 1:3). God creates everything, but also *keeps* it in being by His will. This means that if God took a nap, or forgot about us for a second, the universe would blink out of existence.

Here's a way of understanding this. Imagine in your head, a kitten. Imagine it moving around and playing with string; eating and sleeping and doing all the things that a kitten does. Hold that thought in your head. But also imagine that this kitten is a real, living kitten. It has desires and feelings. It really exists. But the second you stop imagining it, it will cease to exist. That's a lot of responsibility. Most of our pets we have to only remember to feed, walk, and take to the vet once in a while. But this pet you have to think about constantly to keep it alive.

Perhaps some of you have already lost focus and forgotten about your imaginary kitten. Maybe some others will be able to sustain it in being for a few minutes longer. But very soon you will lose focus and forget. And there goes the cat.

THE SON SUSTAINS ALL THINGS BY HIS POWERFUL WORD. -Heb.1:3

Well, we're like this to God. Except God has not forgotten about us. He sustains us all in existence at every moment. We matter so much to Him that He is constantly thinking about us.

From this, we can know a bit more about how much we matter to God. It is not just that He gives us the gift of life once, but He does so at every moment.

And that's something to be truly grateful for.

WHY IS THERE EVIL?

A. God gave us free will to obey and we did not.

Therefore, just as sin entered the world through one man, and death through sin, and in this way death came to all people, because all sinned. —Romans 5:12

As we said before, in the beginning God was living as a Trinity: whole, complete, and perfect. But God *decided* to create as a gift. He whispered, "galaxies," and there were galaxies. He whispered, "pandas," and there were pandas. And he created us, too.

And it was all awesome.

But God wanted something more from humans than He wanted from pandas or star clusters. He wanted *real* relationship. He wanted to have the kind of relationship He had in the Trinity with us.

So, as Genesis 1:27 says, He created humans in His *image*.

Now, the idea of being in God's image has a few different dimensions we need to understand.

First, being in God's image means that we *resemble* God.

This means that when God created humans, He invested them with characteristics that He Himself possesses.

Romans 1:20 teaches that all creation reflects aspects of God's nature. But humans resemble God in special ways. We are given the ability to know God (Colossians 3:10; Psalm 139:14). And in order to know something, we must have some connection to it.

Ostriches and wild donkeys and mountain goats do not know God. But the Bible teaches us that God knows and watches over them (Job 30). The relationship is fairly one-sided.

Humans are different. We are known by God, but can know *Him* as well. And, of course, we can do more than just know God—we should worship Him. True knowledge of a perfect God leads to joyful worship. ✺ This is why the Westminster Catechism's first question says that the main purpose of humans is to "glorify God and enjoy Him forever."

There's another way that humans, created in the image of God, resemble our Creator.

In Genesis 1:26–27, God said, "Let *us* make mankind in our image, in our likeness ... So God created mankind in his own image, in the image of God he created them; male and female he created them" (emphasis mine).

When God refers to Himself, He speaks of Himself as "us." God is not just a single "I," but is, in fact, a Trinity. *A unity that includes difference.*

When God creates humans He makes them in His image as "male and female." *A unity that includes difference.* ✺

Humans resemble God by being different-yet-unified, like the different notes in a chord that combine to make a harmony.

But there's more. Humans not only *resemble* God, but were created to *represent* Him in the world.

Representing God means that God intended for us to be His image in the world. We are meant to be God's *representatives* in the way that United States congressmen (and congresswomen) represent their home districts in Washington D.C. (in the appropriately named House of Representatives). ✴

As I said in the last lesson, the work of being God's image in the world brings with it some responsibilities. Just like a congresswoman has work that she must do as a part of her official duties, so humans were given a task as God's official representatives. As Genesis 1 teaches, humans were meant to rule over creation.

It makes sense then, that when God placed humans in a garden, He gave them some responsibilities. He gave them some things to do, and some things not to do.

He told the humans to tend the garden.

And He told the humans not to eat the forbidden fruit.

He gave them a choice. You can do what I've commanded. That'll be great. Or you can do what I've forbidden, and that'll be terrible.

And what did we do? We did the terrible thing. We broke God's command. And continue to do so today.

Some of you might be thinking: Why did God give humans a chance to mess up? Why did God plant that forbidden tree in the garden? It's crazy. If God had never planted that tree we'd all be living it up, enjoying paradise. Why did God make it possible for the first humans to go wrong?

Well, here's why: *real relationship requires real freedom.*

God didn't just want a nice relationship, like you might have with your dog, He wanted a real relationship, where love is freely given between different people.

Here's an analogy: Imagine you're a young man or woman. You're starting to think about marriage and there's a guy or a girl that you think is the bee's knees. You're *crazy* about them. They're just right. They look just like you want them to look. They act just like you'd want them to act. But they won't give you the time of day. Not interested at *all*.

And now imagine there's a pill—it's called the Cupid Capsule—and you could give this guy or girl the Cupid Capsule and they would instantly fall in love with you and remain in love with you forever.

Would you give them the pill? Most people say, "No, definitely not." Why is that? Well, because most of us understand that real love requires real freedom. If we make someone love us, the very act of compelling them to love negates the very thing we want: the free response of affection.

And this is why God gave us the ability to obey or not.

The problem for us now is, we didn't obey (Genesis 3:6).

And so now we're stuck with the real consequences that come from real freedom.

And, as the Bible teaches, the real consequences of disobeying God are *disrupted relationship* and *death.*

Adam and Eve's disobedience messed up their relationship with the triune God.

Connection and communication were broken—like when phone lines or cell phone towers are destroyed, communication is disrupted. Humans no longer had the full knowledge of God they were supposed to.

Disobedience also destroyed our ability to represent God and carry out our responsibilities. Humans could no longer rule over creation as they were intended to (Genesis 3:17–19).

Instead of unity with God and others, humans were now at odds with each other and God (Genesis 3:16). Instead of enjoying the closeness of family, humans became enemies of God and each other (Romans 5:10).

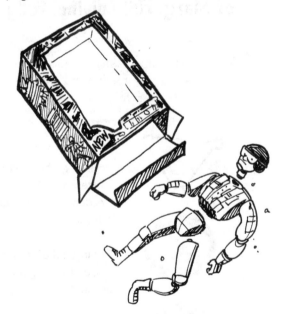

And *death* also entered the human story (Genesis 2:17; Romans 5:14). So now our default setting, when we come out of the box, is already aimed toward death. Cut off from God, the redeeming source of life, we all die.

Now when Jesus comes, He's going to solve both these problems, by restoring our relationship with God and by conquering death. In a word, Jesus restores the *image* of God that we had in the beginning.

WHO IS JESUS CHRIST?

A. The eternally begotten Son of God and the Son of Mary. Fully divine. Fully human.

The Word became flesh and made his dwelling among us. We have seen his glory, the glory of the one and only Son, who came from the Father, full of grace and truth. —John 1:14

As we said before, the story of God goes like this: In the beginning, the Trinity was whole and complete, and then created as a free gift of love. Humans were given *real freedom* and *real responsibility* so there could be *real relationship*.

But instead of responding with the thankfulness we owed to God for the gift of life, the universe, and everything, we ungratefully disobeyed.

And because of our disobedience, our relationship with God was broken, and the punishment that fell on us was death.

But God had a plan.

Through a series of promises and marvelous works, God recreated a people, Israel, who would know God and have relationship with Him.

The story of the Old Testament is that story. Broken relationship and a broken people are brought back into connection with God.

As we discussed before, humans were made in the image of God. They were created to be God's representatives on earth. Through the covenants with Noah, Abraham, Moses, and David, God reestablishes connection with humanity.

In His covenant with Abraham, God picked a man through whom He would create a nation. Abraham would have a son and his children would dwell in the Promised Land (Genesis 12:1-7).

In His covenant with Moses, God chose a man to tell the Israelites how to live as God's people. They would not simply be a nation, but a *holy* nation (Exodus 19:5-6).

Through His covenants, God established a people again. He rebuilt a community that would represent and resemble Him on earth.

But God didn't just want one people, at one place, to have connection to Him; He wanted all people to have connection to Him. This plan was seen even way back in God's covenant with Abraham, where God promised that through Abraham "all the peoples of the earth will be blessed" (Genesis 12:3). ✳

And so the second person of the Trinity, Jesus Christ, came down from heaven to earth to make a permanent connection between God and all of humanity.

One of the key images for this connection is given to us in the Old and New Testaments.

In Genesis 28:12, Jacob dreamed of a ladder that went from heaven to earth and had angels ascending and descending on it.

In John 1:51, Jesus described Himself as that ladder—a ladder that stretched all the way up to the heavens and came all the way down to the earth.

This ladder is perhaps the clearest image for what Jesus did when He became human. Jesus bridged heaven and earth.

Before, the Son was just at the top of the ladder. ✾ And the rest of us were at the bottom of it.

With the virgin birth, Jesus lowered a ladder all the way down and came down to our level (Luke 1:35). ✾

The word that we use to describe Jesus coming down to earth is "incarnation." Incarnation means "taking on flesh."

The incarnation, which we read about in the beginning of the Gospels, describes the way that the Son of God, who was divine spirit, added humanity to who He was.

This means that God is now linked to humanity forever, in the person of Jesus Christ: one person with two natures. In the incarnation, the Son of God had a human nature as well as a divine nature. Jesus was a human kind of thing, and a divine kind of thing. He was both.

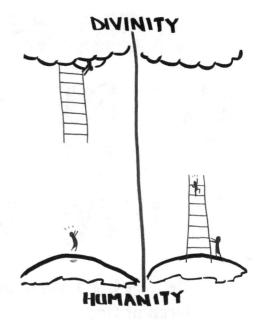

This means that Jesus had everything about Him that was truly human. He had a human mother. A human body. A human will. And human emotions. ✥

But He was also at the same time fully divine. He had a divine father. Divine power. And a divine will.

The mystery of the incarnation is found in this, that both natures (both kinds of thing) were united in one person: the God-Man Jesus Christ. ✥

Here's why this is important. If Jesus wasn't fully human, then He didn't come all the way down, and we can't get on the ladder (Hebrews 2:17).

If Jesus wasn't fully divine, then He can't take us all the way up back to God. We can climb the ladder, but we can't get to where God is (Philippians 2:6-7).

But the amazing thing is that Jesus bridged the gap. In His great humility, the Son of God went all the way from heaven down to earth. He hit the ground with a thud and got dirt on Him. Not only did God become human, He was born into a lowly status. Jesus was a construction worker's son from a one-stoplight town in a tiny oppressed country at the edge of the Roman Empire. He grew up poor. Worked with His hands. Mixed with everyday folks. He ate, drank, laughed, cried, suffered, and died. He took on all that was truly human.

There can be no clearer demonstration of God's love than this. God became a man. So now when we look to God, we see in the Holy Trinity, Jesus Christ, a real human being, staring back at us from the right hand of God the Father, beckoning us up the ladder.

WHY DID THE SON OF GOD BECOME HUMAN?

A. Because God loves us and wants to make us true children of God.

But when the set time had fully come, God sent his Son, born of a woman, born under the law, to redeem those under the law, that we might receive adoption to sonship. —Galatians 4:4–5

Okay, so...

Despite the fact that we were the ungrateful ones...

Despite the fact that we received the gift of life and relationship with God and then rejected the Giver...

Despite the fact that it was we who messed up, God reestablished relationship, loving and caring for the people of Israel, and finally became a human in the person of Jesus Christ.

We broke the connection. But God reestablished it.

The question that we want to ask, though, is, "Why?" Why did God bother? Why didn't God just write us off and go start another planet with more grateful and obedient people?

This question is important because we must remember that God is perfect. And this means that He's perfectly good. A perfectly good person always understands what is wrong and hates it.

God hates sin. And, as the Bible teaches, God would have been perfectly justified in letting us experience the punishment for sin. All have sinned (Romans 3:23). And the wages of sin is death (Romans 6:23).

God could have just let us go.

But He didn't. Again, we ask, "Why?"

Well, the answer here is given in the Bible. God *loves* the world he made (John 3:16). God loves us and isn't willing to write us off when we disobey.

There's a story that most of you are very familiar with from the gospel of Luke.

A father had two sons: an older son and a younger son. And the younger son came to the father and told him he didn't want to be his son anymore and asked for his share of the inheritance. The father gave the son his share of the money and the son left for a far off country, where he blew all the cash partying. Then broke and alone, the son became desperate, and headed back home to ask to be a slave in his father's house. But the father saw the son from afar and ran to meet him. The father threw his best coat and his Rolex watch on the son and took his whole household out to a steakhouse to celebrate. He told his older son, "We have to celebrate and be glad, because this brother of yours was dead and is alive again; he was lost and is found again."

The son was ungrateful to the father. He asked for his money and left. He told the father he didn't love him. But the father never stopped loving the son. And when the son returned the father made him part of the family again.

That's the story Jesus told in Luke 15. The parable of the prodigal (or "wasteful") son.

This story is like our story. We're ungrateful and we abandon God. But God still loves us. Yet in our story God actually goes one step further. He sends His Son out to get us and bring us back. In our story we're still living in that far off country when Jesus comes and finds us, pulls us out of the ditch, and asks us to come home again.

In order to understand why God acts like the father in the story of the prodigal son (in fact, acts even more generously than the father in that story), we have to understand what God's motivation is, and His ultimate goal.

As Scripture clearly teaches, God's *motivation is love*. ✳ Romans 5:8 teaches, "God demonstrates his own love for us in this: while we were still sinners, Christ died for us." The rescue operation God carries out through Jesus is not just a momentary whim on God's part. The incarnation is a demonstration of

something deep in God. God loves us. Love goes so deep in God that the Bible says that God is love (1 John 4:8). God cannot help but be loving. As we discussed before, the Trinity teaches us that love is fundamental to God's very being.

But there's more to it than this. To understand how God loves us, we need to understand the ultimate goal of His love toward us. ✿

God's goal is this: to *make us family*. ✿ As Galatians 4:5 teaches, the purpose of the incarnation is to give us "adoption to sonship." We are to be re-adopted: no longer orphans without a loving father, but true sons and daughters of God.

That was what God wanted in the beginning. God loves us and people want to be with the things they love. God wants us with Him. He wants to have us participate in the life of God as family.

And that goal never changes.

And so when Jesus came, He offered the chance to come back with Him to God's house.

This is the ultimate reason the Son of God became incarnate. *Jesus became like us so we could be His brothers and sisters, with God as our Father.* This is why we read in John 1:12: "Yet to all who did receive him, to those who believed in his name, he gave the right to become children of God."

WHAT IS SALVATION?

A. Through Jesus' sacrificial death and victorious resurrection, we are reconciled with God and rescued from destruction.

For there is one God and one mediator between God and mankind, the man Christ Jesus, who gave himself as a ransom for all people. This has now been witnessed to at the proper time. —1 Timothy 2:5-6

God's *motivation* is love and His *goal* is to make us family again—to have right relationship. But there's a problem, we haven't seen the way that God accomplishes His goal.

Disrupted Relationships

Death

Because of our disobedience, we are left with *disrupted relationship* and *death*. We can't have right relationship with God forever because sin and sin's consequences are an obstacle. So how does God remove this boulder from the path back to Him?

We can think about it like this:

» God's *motivation* is love.
» God's *goal* is making us family again.
» God's way of dealing with disrupted relationship and death is through Jesus' *death* and *resurrection*.

There are two main ways of understanding what Jesus did to save us: *reconciliation* and *rescue*. *Reconciliation* means restoring relationship. *Rescue* means saving us from danger.

Jesus did both. He reconciled us back to God, and He rescued us from evil and death.

So how did He do that?

When there's a rift in a relationship you often have to offer something up to make peace. Maybe it's just an apology, or maybe it's a note or a gift.

Imagine that you went to a friend's house for Thanksgiving dinner and all the food was laid out on the table. The turkey and the stuffing and gravy and the sides and

Reconciliation

Rescue

the desserts. And you decide to try out, for the first time, a magic trick. You're going to try and pull the tablecloth out from under all the food in one swoop. Everybody says don't do it, but you do it anyway and, as you might expect, all the food tumbles down to the floor. The turkey, and the gravy, and the mashed potatoes are all ruined.

Now, in this case you really would have messed up. So you'll need to make it up to your friend. And the best way to do that would be for you to cook a Thanksgiving meal at your house and invite everyone over.

But what if you can't cook? What if you don't have anything to offer to make it up to your friend?

Well that's a little bit like what our situation was with God. We disobeyed God's law but didn't have anything to offer God to make it up to Him.

So Jesus came and offered a sacrifice to God on our behalf. Jesus made it up to the Father by giving Himself as a perfect offering.

This is what happened on the cross. Jesus sacrificed Himself to pay, once and for all, the penalty for our disobedience. He took our place, took our punishment, and offered Himself to the Father (1 John 2:2).

This took care of the disrupted relationship. But it didn't solve the punishment for sin, which was death.

Jesus' resurrection solved this problem. Jesus was killed and then came back to life, as the first example of what will happen to us as well. Jesus showed us that death isn't the end of the story. God's goal to have us as part of His family can't be defeated by death. Because we will be resurrected like Him. ✿

Imagine it a bit like this. Let's say that you and your family have been kidnapped by a mad scientist and kept in his secret fortress. You try everything you can to escape, but everything fails. The government has been trying to free you, but every attempt to attack the base is repelled by the mad scientist's powerful weapons. You're stuck. But you hold out hope because you have a brother who is a top agent in the military. You know that he might be able to save you. Then one day, the guards throw open the prison doors and toss in your last hope: your brother the secret agent. He's so badly beaten he's barely recognizable. You all begin to cry. Your last hope for rescue has been captured. But your brother lurches to his feet and smiles at you. With great pain, he begins to pull lock picks out from under his skin. He gets to work, opens the cell doors, and leads the way to freedom. What seemed like the darkest moment was actually a part of his rescue plan.

This is what Jesus did. In Matthew 16:18, Jesus said that not even the gates of hell will stand against the church. And the way Jesus defeated the enemy of death was in the most unexpected way of all. He defeated death by dying.

Jesus descended to the realm of the dead and broke free again, opening the way for us all.

We might even say, with the nails of the cross Jesus picked the locks of the gates of hell.

This is how Jesus solved our two big problems. He reconciled us back to God by being a perfect sacrifice for our sins, and He defeated the power of death in His resurrection.

THE GATES of HELL WILL NOT OVERCOME IT Mt. 16:18

WHAT IS REQUIRED FOR SALVATION?

A. We must repent and believe in Jesus Christ.

"The time has come," he said. "The kingdom of God has come near. Repent and believe the good news!" —Mark 1:15

There's a word that we use to describe what Jesus did when He reconciled us with God and saved us from the power of death. That word is "salvation." To be saved means to be saved from something. And Jesus saved us from the *disruption* and *destruction* that came from our *disobedience*.

HOW CAN W

The question then, for us, is "How can we be saved?"

The Bible tells us that salvation has two main pieces: *repenting of our disobedience* and *believing in Jesus Christ.*

The word "repent" in the Bible means to change your mind. And the word "believe" in the Bible means to fully trust. ✹

Repentance means that you realize the way you've been doing things isn't working. Your plans have failed and you have to make a change.

Here's what this looks like.

Let's say that you live in a kingdom with a good and righteous king. But you and a group of fellow citizens decide to overthrow the king and become rulers yourselves. So you take up arms and try to take the castle. You fail and retreat to a cave in the mountains where you think about how you can overthrow the king.

You try again and again, but fail each time. Finally, weary and shivering in your cave, you are beginning to doubt your original reasons for rebellion. You're not sure it was a good idea to begin with.

Suddenly you hear a regiment of the king's soldiers approaching. You look out and there they are. All armed to the teeth with the king leading the charge. You're surrounded, outnumbered, and outgunned.

How can you be saved?

The only way to be saved in this case is to wave the white flag. Throw down your weapons, give up being rebels, and surrender. ✸

That's repentance.

Now, it must be said that repentance is never fun. The Bible recognizes this when it describes the feeling that leads to true repentance as "godly sorrow" (2 Cor. 7:10). ✸ It's a moment when you hit rock bottom. It's that sinking feeling when you realize that your plans aren't working. It's bad news.

But there's hope. As Frederick Buechner said, "The gospel is bad news before it is good news." ✸

Believing is what turns everything around. Believing in God takes the next step after repentance. It moves us from rejection of ourselves to following someone better.

This is an important point to understand because sometimes we think that being a Christian is primarily about avoiding sin. It's about saying "no" to the wrong things. And this is true, but it's not the whole story. Christianity is much more about saying "yes" to the right things, which is to say the right person, Jesus, and letting Him rule over your life.

Imagine that you're there in the cave, and the king calls out, "Surrender or be destroyed!" You throw down your weapons and wave the white flag.

The king gets off his horse and comes into the cave. He says, "Have you turned away from your rebellion?" You say you have. "Very well, but there is something more that I need. Being a citizen in this kingdom doesn't just mean not actively rebelling. It means actively serving the king." ✸

So the king asks you to trust him fully. You agree.

"If you trust me fully," the king says, "you must enlist in my army, and help to turn other rebels back to serving me." ✿

That's what belief looks like. It means fully trusting that God's ways are better than our own.

Jesus doesn't just deliver you from your old life, He offers you an entirely new one.

Repent and believe, Jesus said. That's what it takes to let God save us.

WHAT ARE THE BENEFITS OF SALVATION?

A. We are pardoned by God, made part of God's family again, and given resurrection life and power.

Therefore, since we have been justified through faith, we have peace with God through our Lord Jesus Christ. —Romans 5:1

As we said before, sin caused two problems: *disrupted relationship* and *death.*

We were alienated from God, enemies of God, and had fallen victim to the clutches of evil and death. We needed *reconciliation* and *rescue.*

That's what Jesus did—He reconciled us to the Father again on the cross. And He triumphed over death and the devil in His glorious resurrection.

The way that we participate in this *reconciliation* and *rescue* is by *repenting* and *believing.*

Repentance is laying down our rebellious weapons and waving the white flag of surrender.

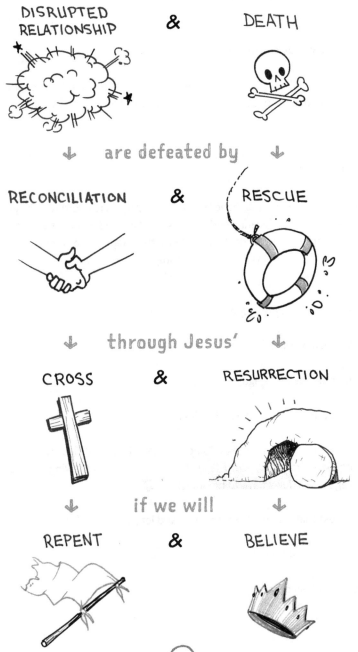

DISRUPTED RELATIONSHIP & DEATH

↓ are defeated by ↓

RECONCILIATION & RESCUE

↓ through Jesus' ↓

CROSS & RESURRECTION

↓ if we will ↓

REPENT & BELIEVE

Believing is trusting the King of the universe completely and joining His side.

All this is review. Here's something new.

If we repent and believe, then we are *pardoned for our sin*, and *given new life again*. This is what happens to us when we respond to Jesus' invitation to repent and believe.

In order to understand pardon and new life, let's return again to that example we heard in the last lesson.

Imagine a group of rebels that have tried again and again to overthrow the good and righteous king. Finally, shivering and starving, the king and his entire army find them in a cave. Except instead of destroying them, the king calls for them to surrender, and they do. And then, even more surprising, he asks them to join his side, and they do.

The rebels in this case are pardoned for their sin.

They're forgiven by the king.

He doesn't hold their sins against them.

And now they are not at war with the king.

This is like what Romans 5:1 says, "since we have been justified by faith we have peace with God through our Lord Jesus Christ." Because of the king's pardon we're at *peace* again. We don't have to be punished. �֍

But it isn't just that the rebels are forgiven and let go.

The king wants something more.

He wants the rebels to join his side.

He wants them to be with him, and to help turn other rebels back into loyal subjects. So the rebels become members of the king's army. And he takes them back and has them sit by the fire to warm up, and feeds them, and clothes them in his colors. The king doesn't just spare them the punishment of death, he gives the rebels new life! As Ephesians 2:5 says, we are "made alive together with Christ." ✴

God isn't just interested in forgiving our *past*, He's about ensuring we have a *future*.

John Wesley, an eighteenth-century preacher, horse rider, and sporter of long, flowing hair, compared salvation to a *house*. ✴ Repentance is like the porch. It's what lets us in the gate. Believing is like the door. It's what gives us access to the family of God again.

But you don't want to just get up to the porch, and then just stand in the doorway. You want to go on in and begin to live in the house. It's inside where the real life happens. That's where the food is, and the fire, and the furniture. That's where God is calling us.

But there's a catch.

Life in the house is good, but if you've ever been to someone else's house you learn that they often do things differently there. They may have different rules. And living in God's house means learning new ways of living. ✴

And that's what we'll talk about in the next lesson.

WHAT HAPPENS WHEN WE LIVE OUT OUR SALVATION IN CHRIST?

A: God continues to work in us to make us holy and blameless.

But now he has reconciled you by Christ's physical body through death to present you holy in his sight, without blemish and free from accusation. —Colossians 1:22

Okay, so there are a few big, fancy words that we use when we talk about salvation. They are:

» Justification
» Regeneration
» Sanctification

We've just been talking in the previous lesson about justification and regeneration (though we didn't use those terms).

Justification is being set right again with God. Making peace with God. It's being forgiven for our rebellion.

Regeneration is the new life that comes from believing in God. It's being welcomed into God's household again where there's food and shelter. And being given the ability to live as faithful servants.

Sanctification is the process of God helping us to work out the last shreds of rebellion from our hearts and minds.

Everything important is worth saying twice, so I'll say this again and put things even more simply:

» *Justification* spares us from death. It is God's action of pardoning us in Christ, so that it is "just as if" we'd never sinned.
» *Regeneration* gives us life. It is God's action of bringing us back from the dead and giving us power to follow Christ.
» *Sanctification* gives us new ways of living. It is God's action of helping us to actually become like Christ.

Through justification and regeneration God has planted in us a seed of new life, where once the soil was dead and barren. Sanctification is "growing in grace" until the plant is fully grown (2 Peter 3:18).

To understand sanctification, it helps to know what the word means. Sanctification means the process of becoming holy, which means to be set apart for its intended purpose. ✴ In our case, that means to do the good works

God planned for us in Jesus Christ (Ephesians 2:10). ✿ In other words, we are meant to be righteous the way that Jesus is righteous.

This is hard.

And we can't do it on our own. But there's good news.

The whole Trinity is on the case.

As 1 Peter 1:2 teaches, the Father has called us to be obedient to the Son, through the sanctifying work of the Spirit.

Sanctification is the work of the Spirit to make us like Jesus, so that we can have perfect relationship with the Father.

This is necessary because we come out of the box, even when we are newly born, with a sinful nature. And we've grown up in a sinful world, among sinful people. Even when we're forgiven and given new life we don't have the understanding or ability to live as members of God's family.

Here's a bit what it's like. Imagine you were lost in the forest as a child and, like Mowgli from *The Jungle Book*, you were raised in the wild by wolves. You learn all the wolfish ways of living and hunting. You learn to fight like a wolf. You survive by killing and hiding food and scaring off other animals to make sure you always have enough to eat.

One day, though, a tiger comes into the forest and you can't fight him off. He's too powerful, so you retreat to your cave, but he corners you. Except just then you hear a gunshot. The tiger runs off, and there are your parents. They've found you at last. And they take you home.

They are overjoyed at your return. And you're glad to be saved, but you find life in the human world confusing. You get in fights with people who come to visit, you steal and hide food from your parents, and you live in constant fear that others will try and kill you. In other words, you are still living in all the ways that you learned in the forest. Those ways may work in the forest, but they don't work in a human family.

You have to go back and learn all the stuff you never learned as a child. You have to learn to bathe (but you're afraid of water), and learn to read (even though it's not as exciting as running around in the woods), and you have to learn to trust other people (which is very hard for you).

Your parents have taken the boy out of the forest—which was hard—but it's turned out to be even harder to take the forest out of the boy.

That's how it is with us and God.

To return to the example of the rebels who become servants of the king, it's the work of a moment to surrender to the king, but it's a long process to stop thinking, and acting, and feeling like a rebel. 3 The king gives us pardon and new life, but it's work to become faithful servants (Romans 6:18, 22)

That's sanctification. It's the work of going from just being saved by Jesus' death to being imitators of Jesus' life.

So if it's so hard and difficult, why does God bother?

Again, going back to why the Father sent His Son Jesus, the reason God saves us and then transforms us, is because He loves us.

C. S. Lewis said it well:

> We are, not metaphorically but in very truth, a Divine work of art, something that God is making, and therefore something with which He will not be satisfied until it has a certain character. Here again we come up against what I have called the "intolerable compliment." Over a sketch

made idly to amuse a child, an artist may not take much trouble: he may be content to let it go even though it is not exactly as he meant it to be. But over the great picture of his life—the work which he loves, though in a different fashion, as intensely as a man loves a woman or a mother a child—he will take endless trouble—and would, doubtless, thereby give endless trouble to the picture if it were sentient. One can imagine a sentient picture, after being rubbed and scraped and recommenced for the tenth time, wishing that it were only a thumbnail sketch whose making was over in a minute. In the same way, it is natural for us to wish that God had designed for us a less glorious and less arduous destiny; but then we are wishing not for more love but for less. God loves us so much he won't be satisfied until we're perfect. ✺

In this way we can be reminded of Leonardo da Vinci, who kept the Mona Lisa with him continually, even when he moved from Italy to France. He loved the painting and wanted it to be great. And so he worked on it for years and years so it would be perfect. ✺

We're like that. We're God's great masterpiece that He started at the beginning, and won't be satisfied until it's just right again. ✺

As Paul wrote in Colossians 1:22, Jesus is working to make us holy and blameless. He's rubbing out all the stains, and repainting the rough lines until the picture is perfect and beautiful.

What this means for us is that as long as we let Him, God will continue to change our hearts and minds until we're totally free from those old rebellious ways.

WHO IS THE HOLY SPIRIT?

A. The eternal Spirit of God, who proceeds from the Father and the Son.

But the Advocate, the Holy Spirit, whom the Father will send in my name, will teach you all things and will remind you of everything I have said to you. —John 14:26

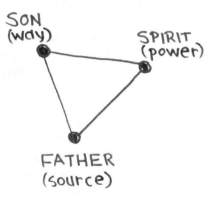

In the first lesson we talked about the Trinity. The Trinity is the most important idea in understanding who God is. The Father is the Source. The Son is the Way. The Spirit is the Power.

We see this role of the Spirit played out all throughout the story of Scripture.

» The Spirit is the breath of life breathed into humans in Genesis 2.
» The Spirit is the power by which the Son is born of the Virgin Mary, as taught by Matthew 1 and Luke 1.
» The Spirit is the power that fills the early church to spread the good news of Jesus in Acts 2.

> » The Spirit breathed life into the writers of Scripture so that it can teach and guide us, as it says in 2 Timothy 3:14-17 and 2 Peter 1:21.

The Spirit is the power of God in us, helping us to follow Jesus back to the Father.

One of the ways that Christians have always described the role of the Spirit is as the *giver of life*. The Spirit is the power of God to bring life to the world and to us. 🔆

But as important as the Holy Spirit is, we often forget to think about the Spirit.

This is because the work of the Spirit is often behind the scenes; He sometimes goes unnoticed. In this way, the Spirit is a bit like the sound technician at a concert. When we go to a concert, our focus is toward the front of the stage, where the musicians are. Rarely do we turn around and notice that the sound guy is back there, making sure everything sounds perfect.

Like a sound guy, the Spirit's work is utterly important, but often invisible. ✡

It makes sense then that one image used all throughout Scripture to describe the Spirit is air, or breath.

Air is all around us, but it's invisible. It gives us life at every second, but we forget that it's there.

Take a second and fill your lungs with air, then blow it out again. If you weren't pumping gas or sitting near a garbage dump, the experience was probably pleasant. You feel calmer, healthier, and more aware of the important life-giving role the air serves. If you try and hold your breath for even just thirty seconds, you'll really start to miss the air.

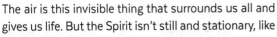

The air is this invisible thing that surrounds us all and gives us life. But the Spirit isn't still and stationary, like the air in a closed-off room. The Spirit moves and has a will of His own. When the air moves it makes wind, which is this uncontrollable force. Jesus said of the Spirit, "The wind blows wherever it pleases. You hear its sound, but you cannot tell where it comes from or where it is going" (John 3:8).

If you've ever been out in a strong wind you know the power that wind has. Wind can tear houses down, or it can generate electricity.

The Spirit's like that. Powerful and life-giving.

» It was a *wind* that parted the Red Sea as the Israelites fled from Egypt.
» It was a *wind* that breathed life into the valley of dry bones in Ezekiel.
» When the Spirit descended on the disciples in Acts 2, it was preceded by the sound of a mighty *wind.*

It makes sense, then, that Hebrew and Greek both use the same word for "wind," "breath," and "spirit." In Hebrew that's *ruach.* In Greek, *pneuma.*

Invisible. Life-Giving. Powerful. That's the Spirit.

WHAT DOES THE HOLY SPIRIT DO?

A. The Spirit leads us to repentance, gives us new life, and empowers us to follow Jesus.

He saved us, not because of righteous things we had done, but because of his mercy. He saved us through the washing of rebirth and renewal by the Holy Spirit, whom he poured out on us generously through Jesus Christ our Savior. —Titus 3:5-6

Now, the Spirit does many things:

» Teaches
» Guides
» Strengthens
» Comforts

As we said before, everything God does, God does as a Trinity. So the Spirit's involved in lots of different things.

But we want to focus on salvation specifically, as a way of understanding how the Spirit works. The Trinity is unified, but the persons all operate differently within any action of God. Jesus opens up to us the "way" of salvation. He makes an offering to the Father in our place, so that we can be reconciled, and He defeats evil and death in His resurrection, so we can be rescued.

As we are saved by the Father, we do so through the way Jesus has made. But we can only do so in the power of the Spirit.

We get to have right relationship with God again because of what Jesus did.

But we only get to participate in what Jesus did through the power of the Spirit.

We talked before about two key things for salvation: repenting and believing. Through waving the white flag of surrender and trusting in the rightful king we have pardon and new life.

Repenting (waving the white flag)
and
Believing (trusting and following the king)

Leads to:

Pardon (forgiveness for our rebellion)
and
New Life (a place and purpose in the king's army)

Now, here's what's cool. Even though it seems like repenting and believing are things that we just decide to do on our own, the Bible says that it's actually the Spirit working through us giving us the ability to repent and believe. We must cooperate with divine grace. But without the Spirit working behind the scenes, we never would have been able to repent and believe in the first place.

The Father is the source. The Son is the way. The Spirit is the power.

It's the Spirit who *leads* us to repent, by convicting us of sin, and then gives us the grace to be able to choose to trust God.

Here's an analogy for what this looks like.

Let's say every now and then your teeth hurt. Not too bad, just a twinge of pain every so often. When you drink something hot or cold it hurts, but you ignore it. Then one day you have to go to the dentist and the dentist says, "Your teeth are riddled

with cavities. We have to do some major drilling." You don't want to have your teeth drilled. That's going to be terrible. You'd rather just put up with the occasional pain. But the dentist shows you some X-rays of how bad your teeth are, and tells you that if you don't get them fixed soon, you'll be in for a lot more pain. You might even lose some teeth.

Finally the hard truth sinks in. Even though they don't hurt all the time, your teeth are in bad shape.

The dentist has led you to the point where you realize you're in trouble. He's made the bad news sink in. He's brought you to the point of surrender.

But the good news is that the dentist also has the power to fix your teeth. He gets out the Novocain and the drill and the filling material and goes to work. And at the end of the day you walk out of the dentist with cavity-free teeth. They no longer hurt when you eat ice cream.

The dentist had to get you to believe the bad news, before he could help you experience the good news.

This is like what the Spirit does. John 16:8 says that when the Holy Spirit comes he will "prove [us] to be in the wrong." The Spirit helps us realize that we're hopeless rebels deserving punishment. That's the bad news.

But then the Spirit shows us the good news: that we can have new life in Christ. And the Spirit washes us and restores us. The Spirit gives us more than new teeth, He gives us new life and power to follow Jesus.

We talked about this new life we receive through Jesus' resurrection. And this is delivered to us by the Spirit. It's the Spirit who connects us to Jesus' victory over death and the devil, like an extension cord that's plugged into that empty tomb, which runs through space and time, and delivers resurrection power.

Another way to think about this is that the Spirit scooped up some of that water from Jesus' baptism, and carries it from the Jordan River to where we are.

Titus 3:5-6 says this well, "[God] saved us, not because of righteous things we had done, but because of [God's] mercy. He saved us through the washing of rebirth and renewal by the Holy Spirit, whom he poured out on us generously through Jesus Christ our Savior."

In this sense, the Spirit hits the reset button on us, rebooting our lives so that we can start again fresh (John 3:5).

The Spirit not only brings us back to life and gives us a fresh start, but also enables us to do far more than we should be able to do. The Spirit gives us the kind of power Jesus had. These gifts of the Spirit are described all throughout the New Testament. They are powerful, and are given to us in different ways at different times, often according to the unique ways that God has made us (1 Corinthians 12:1-11; Romans 12:6-8). ✱

But there's a gift that is given to all of us. Jesus promised to empower us to be His witnesses everywhere. Jesus promised us that the Spirit will enable us to look and be like Him (Acts 1:8).

Because the Spirit is always with us, we can be confident we'll faithfully represent Jesus wherever we go (Luke 12:11-12).

This is the good news: as we are saved by God, the Spirit works in us to help us turn away from our old life and have a new one. The Spirit is the power of God, not just working in the world, but in our lives, to turn us into images of Christ.

WHAT IS THE CHURCH?

A. The church is the community of all true believers, who are Christ's body in the world, continuing the work of the apostles.

There is one body and one Spirit, just as you were called to one hope when you were called; one Lord, one faith, one baptism. —Ephesians 4:4-5

As previously stated, before there was anything, there was a family: the family of the triune God.

This means that love is the most basic fact of the universe.

And the Trinity freely chose to create so there could be more love and more things that have the capacity to freely love.

But humans took the gift of life, and the gift of freedom, and turned it against the Giver. We rebelled and disrupted our relationship with God and incurred the penalty of death.

But God still loved us and wanted us to be family again, and so the Father sent His Son to become a man to establish a new family, with Jesus in charge (Ephesians 5:23).

Being a Christian means being a member of Jesus' family. It means living in God's house and learning God's ways.

If you are part of a family, that means there isn't just a parent in charge, but also a lot of brothers and sisters around. There are other family members you live with. The word that we use for the family of God here, with all these different people in it, is the universal *church*.

And just like living with your own brothers and sisters, life in the church can be tough, because there are so many different kinds of people.

There are people who have been Christians for a long time and brand new Christians, smart people and not-so-smart people, there are old people and young people, and talkative people and quiet people, and charming people and smelly people. But they are all part of God's family.

This is one reason that there's an image that the Bible uses a number of times to capture what it means for us to be the church.

The apostle Paul, in a letter to the Corinthians, compared the church to a body: "Just as a body, though one, has many parts, but all its many parts form one body" (1 Corinthians 12:12). There are the teeth and the inner ear, and the spine and the big toe. All these parts are very different. Teeth and ears and spines do very different things. If they were at a party, they might not have a lot to talk about. But they're all still part of the same body, and are still important. ✳

The family of the church needs all kinds of different parts to be complete. It needs young people and old people and talkative people and quiet people and all the rest. ✿

The other reason that Paul compared the church to Christ's body is that it is through the church that Christ continues the work of the Father in the world. Through the church, Christ is present in the world.

The way it works is a little bit like the movie *Avatar*. In the movie, a man is put into a machine that enables him to control the body of an alien species so that he

can do things on their dangerous alien planet called Pandora. The alien body does what he wants it to do. It walks and talks and rides dragons. But the guy controlling it is somewhere else.

In this way, the church is kind of like Jesus' avatar body. Through us Jesus is still teaching and healing and sacrificing for the world.

To use another example, the church is like an outpost of an invading army. Though the church may be in rebel territory, it obeys the laws and leadership of the king it serves. Through the outpost, the king's will is being done in a hostile land.

Drawing all these ideas together, we can see more clearly the core ideas that help us understand what the church is:

Jesus is the head of the church (Colossians 1:18), *which is made up of many different parts* (1 Corinthians 12:12-26), *so that He can be present in the world* (Ephesians 1:22-23).

Now, some of us may like the idea of following Jesus but we don't love the church. We like the head, but we don't like the body. Because the body is full of flawed and very different people.

But heads aren't meant to be without bodies. That's just creepy.

And some of us love being in the body, we like being part of the community, but we don't like obeying the head. Maybe because the head is telling us to go out into the world and do something difficult.

But a body without a head can't live.

That's why the Bible shows us that to be part of God's family means that we have to take the whole package. We have to be under the lordship of Christ, with the whole community of true believers, continuing Jesus' work in the world.

WHAT ARE THE CHURCH'S SACRAMENTS?

A. Baptism is the holy covenant by which we join the church, and Holy Communion is the church's ongoing act of thanksgiving. Both are means of participating in Jesus' death and resurrection.

Therefore go and make disciples of all nations, baptizing them in the name of the Father and of the Son and of the Holy Spirit, and teaching them to obey everything I have commanded you. And surely I am with you always, to the very end of the age. —Matthew 28:19-20

As we said in the last lesson, the church is Christ's body. He's the head that rules over the diverse community of true believers. The church as a whole is Christ's body in the world. But what does it mean to be part of the church? And what does it mean to be a Christian?

Well, the whole point of being a Christian is to become like Jesus.

As we talked about in Unit 2, humans were created in the *image of God*. This means that we *resemble* God, and also that we *represent* Him.

The way that we do this now is to learn to imitate Jesus. By imitating Jesus—the perfect image of God (Hebrews 1:3)—the image of God is restored in us.

But there's a twist. Imitation sometimes sounds like we're merely trying to copy Jesus in a slavish way—as if Jesus were the original and we're just a photocopy. But God's plan for imitation is more creative than that.

As we said in the last lesson, each of us is different, yet we're all important parts of the one body of Christ. Because we're all different, God's way of imitation is for each person to learn how to become like Jesus in their own *unique way*. To paraphrase Dallas Willard's book *The Divine Conspiracy*, discipleship means becoming who Jesus would be if He were you.

We could think about it a little bit like this. There's this character named James Bond who has been played by all these different actors: Sean Connery and George Lazenby and Roger Moore and Timothy Dalton and Pierce Brosnan and Daniel Craig. And each actor had a different approach to the role. All these guys were James Bond, but each in their own way.

And this is kind of what it's like to follow Jesus. Each of us will learn to imitate Jesus but we'll do so in our own way.

It's also a bit like an assignment given by an art teacher. The art teacher might say, "Paint a landscape." Each of the students can faithfully do the assignment, but they'll do it in their own way. Some will paint the mountains, some will paint the woods, some will paint the ocean. And they'll use different mediums as well: watercolor, or oil paints, or acrylics. There are many ways of completing the assignment.

Imitation of Christ is like this. It isn't an act of copying every *specific detail* of the person of Jesus. It's a creative act that will look different for each of us, because God has created us differently.

But there are some essential things that we need to bear in mind to faithfully do the "assignment" Jesus has given us.

In this section we're going to discuss two of these essential parts of the assignment. These are actions initiated by Jesus that the church centers its life around: we call these the sacraments.

Sacrament means a sacred or special action. And there are two special actions in the life of the church that point to key moments in the life and ministry of Jesus. When we participate in these sacraments we are learning to imitate Jesus and become part of Jesus' story.

One sacrament was shown to us by Jesus at the *beginning* of His ministry, and the other was shown to us at the *end*.

At the very beginning of His ministry, Jesus went down to the river Jordan and was baptized by his cousin John. The Spirit descended and the Father declared His approval (Matthew 3:13-17). But this baptism wasn't just for Jesus. It was for everyone who wanted to follow Him. After His resurrection, Jesus commanded His followers to go to all the nations and baptize them in the name of the Father, Son, and Holy Spirit (Matthew 28:19).

At the very end of His ministry, Jesus gathered His core group of followers and celebrated one last supper with them. He broke bread and shared wine and then compared the bread and wine to His body and blood (Luke 22:13-23). At that time, Jesus told His disciples to break bread and drink the wine together in remembrance of Him.

Jesus practiced these things. And He commanded them of us.

As we imitate Jesus, as we learn to play the role that Jesus wants us to play, then we'll want to do these things.

So what do the sacraments mean in the life of the church?

Baptism is *initiation* into the life of the church. Through baptism, God graciously lets us join the household of believers. It's a one-time thing that we do as we enter the church, much in the way that Joshua only had to cross once through the Jordan River to get to the Promised Land.

Communion, though, isn't just a one time thing. It's something we should do as often as we can in the life of the church. It's a *celebration* that Christians always and everywhere have done regularly—as Jesus taught us.

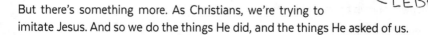

Initiation and celebration. They are what define baptism and Holy Communion.

But there's something more. As Christians, we're trying to imitate Jesus. And so we do the things He did, and the things He asked of us.

In baptism and communion, we're re-enacting key parts of Jesus' life, but we're also participating in Jesus' death and resurrection.

In communion we participate in Christ's death—His broken body and shed blood— and look forward to His return (Matthew 26:26–29).

In baptism, we're buried with Christ under the waters and then raised again.

This was what Jesus called us to. To imitate Him and to follow Him, even to the cross.

The whole life of the church is centered around these two sacraments. We join the church by being buried with Christ. We celebrate Jesus' death as often as we can.

In the life of Christ, the way up always begins by going down (Philippians 2:5–11). We share in Jesus' death so we can share in His resurrection (Romans 8:17). And that's the good news.

WHAT IS THE WORLD'S GREAT HOPE?

A. Christ has died. Christ has risen. Christ will come again to redeem all things and reign as King forever.

He who testifies to these things says, "Yes, I am coming soon." Amen. Come, Lord Jesus. —Revelation 22:20

The Bible tells us a lot of things.

It tells us who God is: God is three persons in one. A Trinity.

It tells us who we are: rebels who have broken God's command and suffer death as a result and who are in need of forgiveness and healing.

But the Bible also tells us something else.

It tells us what time it is.

THE BIBLE TELLS US:

a. who God is

b. who we are

c. what time it is

d. all of the above

Which is to say, the Bible tells us where and when we are in the big story of the world. ✱

» Act 1: The story begins with humans in right relationship to God.
» Act 2: Then the story shifts as humans rebel, and continue to rebel, against God's good rulership.
» Act 3: But God reestablishes relationship through a series of promises to a particular people.
» Act 4: And then God actually enters the world through the incarnation, becoming a man: Jesus Christ. Jesus lives, dies, is raised, and ascends to the Father.

We are now in the part of the story between Jesus' return to the Father and His return back to earth—between the climax of the story and the resolution. God's victory over evil has already happened in Jesus' death and resurrection.

» In the last act of the story, Act 5, the true king works to set everything fully right again through the church, and finally returns to fix everything forever.

In this sense, we are living in the final victorious chapter, but before the very end. We're part of God's clean-up plan, spreading the victory we have through Jesus across the world. ✱ It's a good chapter to live in, but we're also still waiting for God to turn the page in the chapter to the very end. Because that's the best part.

When this happens, when the page finally turns and we finish the last chapter, the goal that God had in the beginning will be fulfilled. God's original plan—to have a people that He can have perfect, loving relationship with—will once again be fully accomplished.

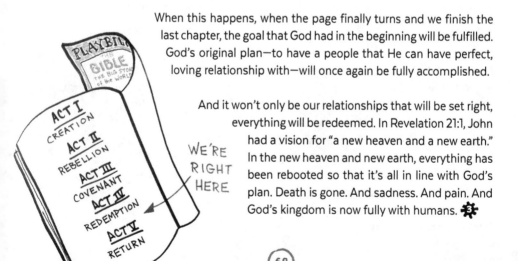

And it won't only be our relationships that will be set right, everything will be redeemed. In Revelation 21:1, John had a vision for "a new heaven and a new earth." In the new heaven and new earth, everything has been rebooted so that it's all in line with God's plan. Death is gone. And sadness. And pain. And God's kingdom is now fully with humans. ✱

This is why John described the holy city descending onto the earth. God's dwelling is with people again.

In a sense, then, the return of Christ and the redemption of all things is an answer to part of one of the most famous prayers in the church. In the Lord's Prayer, we pray, "Thy kingdom come, Thy will be done." We pray for that to happen in partial ways now, but at Jesus' return, it will happen in *full.*

Imagine two circles.

One is the fallen world and one is God's kingdom.

Because Jesus has come and established the church there are some places where the circles overlap, like on a Venn diagram. That's God's kingdom on earth. Right now, the circles just overlap *partially.*

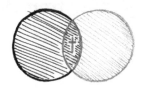

But when Jesus returns, the two will overlap *fully.* There won't be one tiny bit of our circle that isn't completely covered by God's. The two will be made one again, just like it was in the beginning.

THY KINGDOM COME. THY WILL BE DONE.

WHAT IS OUR FUTURE?

A. Like Jesus, we will be raised from the dead, either to worship God forever or to be forever separated from Him.

By his power God raised the Lord from the dead, and he will raise us also.
—1 Corinthians 6:14

What happens to us after we die?

One of the most important questions in life is, "*What happens to us after we die?*"

Sometime when we think about life after death we imagine floating around like ghosts, with wings, up on a cloud where there's a lot of hymns playing and everything is decorated with the color yellow. 🌼 But the Bible teaches that what happened to Jesus after He died is what will happen to all who follow Him.

First Corinthians 15:23 describes Jesus as the "firstfruits"—the first example—of what will happen to those who belong to Jesus.

Jesus wasn't just raised *spiritually* in some sense, but he was raised bodily.

His whole being was raised again to life. His body wasn't in the tomb anymore. After Jesus was raised, He talked with people, walked around, and ate fish (Luke 24:42).

What happened to Jesus will happen to us too, if we're in Him. God will finally defeat the problem of death by raising us to new and eternal life.

This is the final step in salvation. In previous units we talked about *justification*, *regeneration*, and *sanctification*. The last step is *glorification* (Philippians 3:20-21).

Glorification is when the full image of God is restored in us. As we talked about in the lession of Question 4, being in God's image means that we resemble God, and also that we *represent* Him. Sanctification is the process of becoming more holy so that we can resemble God in the way that we live and represent Him on earth. But our bodies and minds do not resemble God in the way He intended. We're still weak, prone to make mistakes, and we're still slowly dying.

When we are resurrected, our whole being (body, soul, and mind) will be put right again. In fact, we'll be better than humans were originally. We'll have perfected bodies.

What's more, as we heard about in the last lesson, God will also redeem all creation, so we'll have a new earth to inhabit with God's kingdom being fully realized on earth.

Again, the *good news* is that everything that happened to Jesus will happen to us, if we're part of His family.

But the *bad news* is that the only alternative to life in Christ is eternal death and unhappiness apart from Him. The good future God has for us and the world is a future where we can have right relationship with the triune God. But only those who will let the triune God save them can participate in God's eternal kingdom.

Because God is the only source of life and happiness, the inevitable result of rejecting God is destruction and misery. ✱

Imagine it a bit like this: Let's say that in your kitchen the appliances could all think and talk. You come in one day to make a smoothie but the blender is unplugged. You plug it in and the blender turns on, but when it does, the blender tells you that it doesn't want to be plugged in. It doesn't like having a plug and it doesn't like having electricity coursing through it. And it doesn't like making smoothies. And it yanks out the cord and turns itself off. When it's unplugged it can't work, or do anything. The next day you plug it back in, but it scowls at you and unplugs itself. You try and talk some sense into the blender, but it won't listen. The other appliances try to convince the blender, but it won't listen to them either. Each time you plug it in, the blender unplugs itself. Finally, after weeks of this, you give up. You put the blender out in the trash and go get a new blender.

This is kind of like what it means to reject God.

God is the source of all life and purpose for us. If we reject the power and purpose that created us, destruction and misery are the only possible results.

Now, this doesn't mean that if we reject God we'll simply cease to exist. Even those who reject God's love will be resurrected, but only for judgment, and then eternal damnation (John 5:29). ✱

The good news, though, is that it doesn't have to be that way.

Through Jesus Christ, the Father offers us a chance to have right relationship and eternal life.

The disruption of sin and the curse of death don't have to win.

God has the power and the desire to overcome these in our lives. And He will do so, if we will allow His grace to work in us.

We are rebels who have rejected God's rule, but the King returns and offers us a chance for forgiveness and life with Him. Not just for a little while, but forever.

NOTES

1 There are a number of places where the church has clarified the right way to speak about God's Trinitarian being. One example is the Athanasian Creed. Another is the statement produced by the Eleventh Council of Toledo, which met in AD 675. This council offered an official explanation of the Trinity, which has been deeply formative for Western theology. The Council of Toledo says this on the Trinity:

> Nor can it properly be said that in the one God there is the Trinity; rather, the one God *is* the Trinity. In the relative names of the persons, the Father is related to the Son, the Son to the Father, and the Holy Spirit to both. While they are called three persons in view of their relations, we believe in one nature or substance. Although we profess three persons, we do not profess three substances, but one substance and three persons [emphasis mine]. (Cited in Alister McGrath, ed. *The Christian Theology Reader*, 4th ed. [Oxford: Wiley-Blackwell, 2011], 176.)

2 Jeremy Begbie's work brought this musical analogy to my attention.

3 The notion that God has always been Father, Son, and Spirit challenges our thinking a bit because any of us who are parents *come to be* parents at some point in our lives. We weren't always someone's parent (though we were always someone's child). But God is different in this way.

Gregory of Nazianzus, an eastern bishop, recognized this challenge a long time ago (way back in the fourth century). In answer to the question, "Can anyone be a 'father' without beginning to be one?" Gregory offered this response:

> Yes, [there can be a father who did not begin to be one, so long as it is] one who did not begin his existence. What begins to exist begins to be a

father. *He* [God the Father] did not later begin to be Father—he did not begin at all. He is "Father" in the true sense, because he is not a son as well. Just as the Son is "Son" in the true sense, because he is not a father as well. In our case, the word "father" cannot be truly appropriate, because we must be fathers *and* sons—the terms carry equal weight. We also stem from a pair [father and mother], not a single being, making us be divided and become human beings gradually, and maybe not even human beings of the kind we are intended to be. (Gregory of Nazianzus, "Oration 29," in *On God and Christ* [Crestwood, NJ: St Vladimir's, 2002], 72–73.)

In addressing the difference between God the Father and human fathers, Gregory cleverly flipped the challenge on its head. It is not that God the Father isn't really a true father because He doesn't begin to be a father at some point, but rather it is we human fathers who aren't "true fathers" because we are also just as truly sons. The Father is a *pure* father. The Son is a *pure* son. And they have always been like this. Human parenthood is just a dim reflection of what God is in the truest form.

Because God is eternal, our brains strain to think about how this relationship of Father and Son has always been so. C. S. Lewis gave the analogy of two books, one of which has always been sitting on the other. The bottom book "causes" the top book to be in the position that it is, but not in a way that created things have causes in time.

In time, causes and effects often follow in chronological succession. Lewis gave this example, "you eat the cucumber first and have the indigestion afterwards." But, as Lewis goes on to say, "it is not so with all causes and results" (C. S. Lewis, *Mere Christianity* [New York, NY: HarperOne, 2001], 172).

Lewis extended the metaphor of the two books to make his point,

> I asked you just now to imagine those two books, and probably most of you did. That is, you made an act of imagination and as a result you had a mental picture. Quite obviously your act of imagining was the cause and the mental picture the result. But that does not mean that you first did the imagining and then got the picture. The moment you did it, the picture was there. Your will was keeping the picture before you all the time. Yet

that act of will and the picture began at exactly the same moment and ended at the same moment. If there were a Being who had always existed and had always been imagining one thing, his act would always have been producing a mental picture; but the picture would be just as eternal as the act. . . . In the same way we must think of the Son always, so to speak, streaming forth from the Father, like light from a lamp, or heat from a fire, or thoughts from a mind. He is the self-expression . . .

 Lewis, *Mere Christianity*, 174.

Baptism is the sacrament that gives us grace for a new life in Christ. And if the whole Trinity is *named* in our salvation, so the Trinity must be at *work* in our salvation.

For more on this, read Thomas Oden, *Classic Christianity: A Systematic Theology* (New York, NY: Harper Collins, 1992), book 1, chapter 5.

One of the oldest creeds of the church, the Apostle's Creed, is affirmed by Christians everywhere. Though the creed nowhere uses the term "Trinity," it affirms the Trinity in its very structure, and tells the story of Scripture in a very simple, accessible way:

I believe in God, the *Father* Almighty, creator of heaven and earth.

I believe in Jesus Christ, his only *Son*, our Lord, who was conceived by the Holy Spirit, born of the Virgin Mary, suffered under Pontius Pilate, was crucified, died, and was buried; he descended to the dead. On the third day he rose again; he ascended into heaven, is seated at the right hand of the Father, and will come again to judge the living and the dead.

I believe in the *Holy Spirit*, the holy catholic [or universal] church, the communion of saints, the forgiveness of sins, the resurrection of the body, and the life everlasting. Amen.

A helpful way of thinking about the structure of the creed is well said by Luke Timothy Johnson: "The creed does not propose a philosophy of life but tells a story with characters and a plot. It is a story about God and the world, about God's investment in humans and their future" (Luke Timothy Johnson, *The Creed: What Christians Believe and Why it Matters* [New York, NY: Doubleday, 2003], 58).

The story of the world told by the creeds is about the Trinity creating and redeeming us. The Father creates, the Son redeems us through His incarnation, death, and resurrection, and the Spirit empowers us to be the body of Christ.

If we had to map the creed onto a shape, it would be the shape of a "V." The movement of God through creation and incarnation is downward, ending at the lowest point (Jesus' death), from there God brings us back up with Jesus with resurrection power and joy through the Spirit, back to the Father.

The truest story we can tell about the world is the story of the Trinity's activity in the world.

UNIT 1 / QUESTION 2: WHAT IS GOD LIKE?

One helpful idea for thinking about how we speak of a perfect being was discussed by Thomas Aquinas, a thirteenth-century Catholic theologian and priest. Aquinas argued that when we use human words to speak about God, we cannot do so in a way that implies they are used in exactly the same way (*Summa Theologica* 1a.13). The word "wise" means the same thing when we say "Solomon is wise" and "God is wise." But the *way* that we use the word "wise" is different.

When we use human words to speak about God, we use them "analogously." An analogy uses a word from its usual situation to apply to a different situation: for instance, when I say that the sandpaper is "rough," and also that my trip to the driver's license office was "rough." The word means the same thing, but it is used in a different way. In the first case, I mean that it is unpleasant and irritating to the touch. In the second, I mean that it was a generally unpleasant and irritating experience. Describing the trip to get my driver's license renewed as "rough" stretches the meaning of the word out of its usual usage to helpfully describe a different kind of experience.

Here's another example. I could describe my lunch as "healthy" and also a famous athlete as "healthy." The word has the same basic meaning, they both relate to being a healthy person. But the way they are used is different. A lunch is healthy because it contributes to my body's health (even if I am actually unhealthy for other reasons). An athlete is healthy because he truly has a healthy body.

So when we speak about God our words stretch. They reach beyond their usual way of describing things. Describing God as "wise" doesn't mean the exact same thing as describing a human as wise. But it also doesn't mean something completely different.

Though it might seem like having to speak of God analogously (which is to say, by using analogy) is less true somehow than speaking using perfectly exact language, we must remember that God Himself affirms the use of analogies to communicate truth. All throughout the Old and New Testaments God very clearly affirms the use of images and stories to help our minds to stretch to understand Him.

For instance, Psalm 62:2 describes God as a "rock." Obviously this doesn't mean that God is a hardened mineral, but rather describes something of God's solidity. God is a firm foundation on which we can rely.

Likewise, Psalm 23 describes God as a "shepherd." Again, we aren't meant to understand this to literally mean God's primary occupation is raising animals for wool and mutton. Rather, this shows us by analogy something about God's character. God loves us and cares for us *like* a shepherd cares for his flock of sheep.

Jesus, at many points in His ministry, used analogies to help us understand the kingdom of God. A common phrase that begins Jesus' parables is "the kingdom of heaven is *like*." The word "like" shows us that Jesus is about to use an analogy. He used concepts that we understand from this world to understand the deep things of God.

For instance, in Matthew 13:45–6, Jesus said, "The kingdom of heaven is like a merchant looking for fine pearls. When he found one of great value, he went away and sold everything he had and bought it." Jesus wasn't telling us all to invest in pearls, He was telling us that the kingdom of God is so valuable that it is worth everything we have.

Aquinas's helpful point about how we use language analogously to speak about God is affirmed in the very words of Jesus. Because God is so much bigger, deeper, and more perfect than we are, our language has to stretch in order to talk about Him. The good news is that God Himself has affirmed using language this way. It is not we who stretch up to Him first. He first stretched down to us by speaking about Himself in ways we could understand. As John Calvin said,

> [A]s nurses commonly do with infants, God is wont in measure to "lisp" in speaking to us. . . . Thus such forms of speaking do not so much express clearly what God is like as accommodate the knowledge of him to our slight capacity. To do this he must descend far beneath his loftiness. (Calvin, *Institutes*, Book 1, Chapter 13, Section 1)

To translate what Calvin is saying a bit: God "baby talks" to us—which is a fitting way for a loving father to speak to his children.

2. Now, some people have noticed that having infinite powers raises certain questions about what God can and can't do. If God is perfectly good, but also perfectly powerful, does this mean that God has the power to tell lies? If God *can* lie, it would seem that He's not necessarily perfectly good. If God *can't* lie, then it would seem God is not perfectly powerful. Either way we have a potential problem.

These questions have led many theologians to add some clarifying statements to what God's abilities really are. For instance, what we mean by "God can do anything" is that "God can do anything logically possible." It may be that there are nonsensical things we can speak of, which God can't do, but only because they are actually meaningless statements.

C. S. Lewis quips in *The Problem of Pain*, "[God's] omnipotence means power to do all that is intrinsically possible, not to do the intrinsically impossible. You may attribute miracles to him, but not nonsense . . . meaningless combinations of words do not suddenly acquire meaning simply because we prefix to them the two other words 'God can'" (C. S. Lewis, *The Problem of Pain* [New York, NY: HarperCollins, 1996], 18).

One example of a nonsensical statement is, "God can create a square circle." This seems to make sense on a first viewing, because this sentence is coherent according to the rules of English grammar. But on a deeper inspection it doesn't make sense, because squares and circles have contradictory natures. For instance, squares have right angles and circles don't. A square circle is logically impossible, and is therefore nonsensical, and is therefore actually meaningless.

Asking if God can make a square circle is the equivalent of asking, in some sort of silly Dr. Seussian language, "Could God furdly glurble a blurble?" The answer to this nonsense question can't be "yes" or "no," because we haven't even asked a meaningful question.

Returning now to the question of whether God can lie or not, we can understand a bit more why it isn't a sensible question to ask of a perfect being. Asking if God can lie is equivalent to asking if a perfectly good being could also be evil? It's the same as asking—"Could God perform an evil-good action?"—which, of course, is nonsense.

UNIT 2 / QUESTION 3: WHAT DID GOD MAKE?

Theologians have a fancy phrase for this view of creation: *ex nihilo* (which means "out of nothing" in Latin). Creation out of nothing contrasts with a common pagan view that the material of the universe always existed. Against this view, most Christian theologians have held to the view that God brought matter into being by His power.

The Christian notion that God created everything has the benefit of philosophical coherence. If God did not create matter, and the material of the universe has always existed, this suggests that the universe is a 'necessary thing.' It must exist. But the universe is made of all kinds of unnecessary things: things that could just as well have not existed (like you and me, and even stars and planets). Anything that exists we can imagine not existing. So, the whole universe is composed of unnecessary things. This suggests that the universe itself is not necessary.

When we compare the notion of God (a perfect being) and the universe, which seems more likely to be the necessary thing? God is a much better candidate for necessity.

Though the idea of an eternally existing material world had some measure of plausibility for the pagans (and is endorsed in a different way by many people today), the idea of creation out of nothing, by a necessary God, has much greater philosophical strength.

2. The beautiful order of the world is clearly on display in the first chapter of Genesis, as God creates and then organizes the different spheres of creation. The first three days of creation God separates light and dark, sky and sea, then water and land. During the second three days He fills them with beautiful creations (stars; fish and birds; wild and domestic creatures), and then sets governors over the spheres (sun and moon over the day and night; humans to govern the earth's land, sea, and sky).

There are two important points to understand about God's pattern in creation here: one is that He fills His creation with beautiful variety. The second is that He puts this incredible variety under governorship. Without order, endless variety can descend into chaos. Humans are called to participate in maintaining God's bountiful creation by shepherding it.

It is at this task that humans failed in the beginning. We failed to keep things in their proper order by putting ourselves above God by disobeying, but also by allowing lower things to become the boss. (For instance, it is worth noting that humans fail to "rule over" the animals, as God commands in Genesis 1:28, by listening to an animal: the snake!)

Every great work of art not only needs to have beautiful material, but also an artist to bring the pieces together into a lovely organized whole.

Humans were supposed to be the ones to maintain the beauty of the world, but we failed. Only in Jesus do we have one who can once again put all creation under His rule. As the Gospels show us, Jesus asserts this rightful rule by having winds, waves, animals, and trees obey Him (see Mark 4:41; Matthew 17:27; and Mark 11:12–25)!

3. Colossians 1:6 and John 1:3 deepen our understanding of Jesus' role in creating the world. The importance that Jesus is the agent of creation—the Word—by which God spoke the world into being, cannot be overstated.

As John 1:11 teaches, the Son "came to that which was his own." He came to *His* world, the world *He* had made, and which *He* aimed to redeem. The incarnation of Jesus (the Word becoming flesh) was nothing strange to the Son. Like a builder making a house he plans to live in, the Son had made a world (with humans capable of bearing His image) that could house Him.

This helps to explain why it is that it is the Son who becomes incarnate. As the agent of creation, He is the one whose Trinitarian role it is to redeem the world. (We will talk about this idea more later, when we discuss the incarnation.)

4. Just as the Son was involved in the creation of the world, so too was the Holy Spirit. Genesis 1:2 teaches that the Spirit of God was present at the creation, "hovering" over the deep. Likewise, Psalm 33:6 says, "By the word of the LORD the heavens were made, their starry host by the breath of his mouth." As we will discuss later, the Hebrew word for "breath" is the same word used for "Spirit" and "life."

Saint Basil the Great, a fourth-century theologian, argued very clearly that creation was accomplished, not just through the Father and the Son, but also through the Spirit: "The Originator of all things is One: He creates through the Son and perfects through the Spirit" (St. Basil the Great, *On the Holy Spirit* [Crestwood, NJ]: St. Vladimir's, 1980], 62).

Just like with our salvation, the Spirit *brings to life* all that the Son has made possible, according to the will of the Father (John 3:5; 6:63). As the Nicene Creed declares, the Spirit is the "giver of life."

Though it may seem to us now a rather uncontroversial idea that the world is good—living in an age where things like environmental conservation are taken as a given—this was not the case for the early church. In fact, many early Christian theologians had to fight against the idea that the created world was an evil thing.

Saint Augustine, one of the most famous theologians of the church, fell under the spell of Manichaenism for a period. Manichaenism, like many other philosophies of the ancient world, believed that the world had been created by an evil deity. Salvation consisted in figuring out how to escape the material world around us. Augustine came to reject this view, and came to understand that everything God creates, from humans down to the lowest gnat, was created good. Sin has corrupted creation, but not wholly destroyed the goodness of the material world.

God loves the material world. He has a plan to redeem it. And the clearest sign of God's love of matter is the incarnation. The Son becomes human, linking the physical with the spiritual and restoring it to its original beauty.

God also shows his love of the material world by using so many physical things He has created in the life of the church. Bread, wine, and water (physical things) are given a spiritual role through the sacraments. Saint John of Damascus, an early medieval theologian, says this well—speaking of how God's use of the physical world in the life of the church shows his love for His material creation:

> Is not the ink and the all-holy book of the Gospels matter? Is not the life-bearing table, which offers us the bread of life, matter? . . . And, before all these things, is not the body and blood of my Lord matter? . . . Do not abuse matter; for it is not dishonorable; this is the view of the Manichees. The only thing that is dishonorable is something that does not have its origin from God, but is our own discovery, by the free inclination and turning of our will from what is natural to what is unnatural, that is sin. (St. John of Damascus, *Three Treatises on the Divine Images* [Crestwood, NJ: St. Vladimir's, 2003], 29–30)

Giving thanks is more than just something we do in ordinary life. It is also the central action of Christian worship. The celebration of Holy

Communion is also called the Eucharist, which literally means "thanksgiving." In many Christian traditions, the pastor or priest will take the wine and bread and lift them upward before celebrating communion. This action of lifting up is like the action of writing the thank-you note. It is a way of showing God that we are thankful for all His blessings. We are thankful for the food and drink that He has given us. Even more so, we are thankful that He has given us salvation through the body and blood of His Son.

Like writing the thank-you note, the action of Christian worship is a sacrifice. Worship requires a sacrifice of our time. Worship requires a sacrifice of our resources. Through these sacrifices we show God our thankfulness for the great gift (and the great sacrifice) He has made for us.

(For more on this read Alexander Schmemann's *For the Life of the World* [Yonkers, NY: St. Vladimir's, 1972].)

 G. K. Chesterton, *Orthodoxy*, "The Ethics of Elfland."

UNIT 2 / QUESTION 4: WHY IS THERE EVIL?

Saint Athanasius, in *On the Incarnation*, focuses on the rationality given to humans, which reflects the rationality of the second person of the Trinity, the Word (which in Greek, is logos, and means "reason").

Having the mental powers to know God is a sign of our being created in the likeness of the *Logos* that made us. To put it simply, humans reflect God's nature partly by having the ability to *reflect*.

Athanasius writes,

> [O]f all things upon earth he had mercy upon the human race, and seeing that by the principle of its own coming into being it would not be able to endure eternally, he granted them a further gift, creating human beings not simply like all the irrational animals upon the earth but making them

according to his own image (cf. Gen. 1:27), giving them a share of the power of his own Word, so that having as it were shadows of Word and being made rational, they might be able to abide in blessedness, living the true life which is really that of the holy ones in paradise (Athanasius, *On the Incarnation.* [Yonkers, NY: St. Vladimir's, 2011], 52)

This special capacity of humans to reason enables us to know God and follow His commands. Following God's commands is of utmost importance for Athanasius because it is by obedience that humans will be able to remain in a state of eternal, joyful life.

In this way, Athanasius ties together two key themes of this lesson. Our knowledge of God is necessary to enjoy life in Him. Rationality is necessary for immortality. Because of the knowledge and rationality given to us by God, we can know Him and His commands. Disobedience of God's commands leads to death.

Theologians through the ages have different views on the meaning of the "image of God." Some—like Irenaeus, Athanasius, and Thomas Aquinas—have rooted it in the rationality and/or the will of the human person. John Calvin rooted the image of God in the soul. For John Wesley, the image of God was in our holiness. All of these accounts seem to be true insofar as they push us to understand our resemblance to God, and the special purpose of humans apart from other creatures. We are given special ability to reflect God and to reflect on God's nature; to know and love Him.

But they do not tell the whole of the biblical story.

Recent theologians like Karl Barth have pushed to re-embrace the biblical account of what the image means by unpacking the text of Genesis 1:26–27. In this text, Barth saw a focus on the sexual difference of humans: their maleness and femaleness (cf. Karl Barth, *Church Dogmatics*, trans. G. Bromiley [Edinburgh: T. & T. Clark, 1960], III.2.). He wrote,

> If there is to be a knowledge of man and woman . . . it will most certainly have to be a form of knowledge which rests upon secure foundations. That man and woman—in the relationship conditioned by this irre-

versible order—are the human creature of God and as such the image of God and likeness of the covenant of grace—this is the secure theological knowledge with which we ourselves work and with which we must be content. What God's command wills for man and woman is that they should be faithful to this their human nature and to the special gift and duty indicated by it. (Ibid., III.4.)

As I said above, being created in the image of God as male and female not only tells us about who God is, but also, for Barth, tells us that the male and female nature of humanity is part of God's command for us. Honoring our unity-with-difference is an essential element of what it means to live faithfully as humans in God's world.

3 Jason Hood, in his recent book, *Imitating God in Christ*, pointed out that it is strange that God allows Israel to share many aspects of the religions of its idolatrous neighbors ("circumcision, a temple, sacrifices, hymns, pilgrimages, ritual feasts, a holy calendar, worship on mountains"), but not the creation of idols (Jason B. Hood, *Imitating God in Christ: Recapturing a Biblical Pattern* [Downer's Grove, IL: InterVarsity Press, 2013], 19).

Why God forbids this one element seems strange until we understand that God has not forbidden the existence of idols (or images) of Himself, but only the creation of new ones.

The "idols" already exist. *We* are the idols. We are not to be worshiped, but we are to play the role that idols play. We are to be the visible representatives of God in the world.

Drawing on Genesis 1 (as I have done above), Hood argued,

When God created humanity, he made us to be his image-bearing idols. (Elsewhere in the Old Testament the word that is here translated "image" usually refers to idols that represent gods or kings.) Seen in this light, God's prohibition is not about his opposition to images but the creation and worship of a lifeless representation of God or false gods. Instead, God makes image-bearers who reflect his glory. . . . [H]umans are God's royal representatives, imaging the one true God as we rule over the world he created. (Ibid., 20)

Humans are meant to be God's designated "ambassadors" in the world, invested with divine authority to rule over creation.

Now, this divine authority is immediately forsaken in the garden, and even when reestablished partially through the Old Testament covenants, is often abandoned or abused. It is only fully reestablished with Jesus who becomes *the* "express image" of God (Hebrews 1:3), who then invests humans once again with the ability to rightly carry out the rights and responsibilities of being God's image.

We can see this reinvestment of ambassadorship, among other places, in Jesus' words in Matthew 28:18–20:

> All authority in heaven and on earth has been given to me. Therefore go and make disciples of all nations, baptizing them in the name of the Father and of the Son and of the Holy Spirit, and teaching them to obey everything I have commanded you. And surely I am with you always, to the very end of the age.

By "real freedom" I mean the ability of a person's will to truly choose. We are not meaningfully free to choose if we don't have it within our power to respond to God or not. Now, this does not mean that humans possess freedom naturally, apart from God's grace. God's grace enables the ability to choose rightly or wrongly.

C. S. Lewis pointed out how our *ability* to choose is nothing to be especially proud of, as if it were something we naturally possess.

> Every faculty you have, your power of thinking or of moving your limbs from moment to moment, is given you by God. If you devoted every moment of your whole life exclusively to His service you could not give Him anything that was not in a sense His own already. So that when we talk of a man doing anything for God or giving anything to God, I will

tell you what that is really like. It is like a small child going to its father and saying, "Daddy, give me sixpence to buy you a birthday present." Of course, the father does, and he is pleased with the child's present. It is all very nice and proper, but only an idiot would think that the father is sixpence to the good on the transaction. (C. S. Lewis, *Mere Christianity* [New York: HarperCollins, 2001], 143)

John Wesley's theology is also helpful for explaining how God's grace empowers us to respond to God's invitation. Using the term "prevenient grace" or "preventing grace," John Wesley argues that some degree of God's grace is with everyone. And it is this grace that acts as a foundation from which humans can respond to God's call.

For Wesley, "prevenient grace" acts like medicine for a sick person. It alleviates some of the symptoms of the fall, but without curing the root disease: sin. Humans are able to choose to perform good actions (or not) because God is still keeping this ability alive in us.

Drawing on John 1:9, which describes the Son as "the true light that gives light to everyone," Wesley argues that all people are not as totally corrupt as they could be without God's ongoing support:

> For allowing that all the souls of men are dead in sin by nature, this excuses none, seeing there is no man that is in a state of mere nature; there is no man, unless he has quenched the Spirit, that is wholly void of the grace of God. No man living is entirely destitute of what is vulgarly called "natural conscience." But this is not natural; it is more properly termed "preventing grace" [or prevenient grace]. Every man has a greater or lesser measure of this . . . Everyone has sooner or later good desires, although the generality of men stifle them before they can strike deep root or produce any considerable fruit. Everyone has some measure of that light, some faint glimmering ray, which, sooner or later, more or less, enlightens every man that cometh into the world. (John Wesley, "On Working Out Our Own Salvation")

It is important to bear in mind that for fallen and sinful people like us, merely having prevenient grace is not enough to complete the work God has for us. We must use the gift of a free will to respond to the call of salvation.

The grace of salvation provides the cure for the disease that is killing us.

Without responding to Jesus' call to repent and believe (which again, we can only do because God gives us the ability to respond) we will never be able to enjoy the abundant life Jesus offers.

The example of the Cupid Capsule is borrowed from Jerry Walls and Scott Burson's book, *C. S. Lewis and Francis Schaeffer* (Downer's Grove, IL: InterVarsity Press, 1998), 239.

UNIT 3 / QUESTION 5: WHO IS JESUS CHRIST?

Sometimes, reading the Old Testament, we can lose sight of the underlying pattern of God's plan, and how it connects to the New Testament. It is easy to get lost in Old Testament lists of genealogy or chapters with specific laws about what foods to eat. But there is a story God is telling.

The story is centered around the creation of a new family. In the Old Testament, God makes His covenants through a particular person (Noah, Abraham, Moses, and David), but the promises extend to an entire people.

- With Noah, it is God's promise to humanity not to destroy it by flood (Genesis 9:11).
- With Abraham, it is to create a people with a specific place to live (Genesis 12:1–7).
- With Moses, it is to be the God of Israel, a holy nation ("a kingdom of priests") with special access to God (Exodus 19:5–6).
- With David, it is to establish an eternal king over Israel (2 Samuel 7).

An underlying pattern is this: through a *promise* to a *person*, God creates a *people*.

The biblical picture of a family, with a father at the head and the household under his protection, offers us a sense of what God is doing. God is rebuilding the representative role that Adam was supposed to play as the head of God's people on earth.

Though most of the covenants were focused on Israel, God's plan was always wider than Israel. We see this in His covenant with Abraham, to make a nation through whom *all people* will be blessed.

When Jesus comes, He will fulfill the purpose of these covenants by establishing a "new covenant" (Luke 22:7–23). This new covenant places Jesus at the head of the new family, which is not just composed of the descendents of Abraham but is for all the earth.

With Jesus, the pattern of the covenants is completed. Through a person (Jesus), God creates a people. He is everything that Noah, Abraham, Moses, and David were, and more.

- He is a new Savior of the human race.
- He is a new Father of many nations and a blessing to the whole earth.
- He is a holy High Priest who puts us directly in connection with God.
- He is an everlasting King.

The Old Testament establishes the pattern that Jesus will fulfill in the New Testament.

(For more on this, check out Sandra Richter, *The Epic of Eden* [Downer's Grove, IL: InterVarsity Press, 2008].)

One of the greatest battles ever fought in the church was over the issue of whether Jesus was fully divine. A third-century priest named Arius argued that Jesus Christ did not have a fully divine nature, but only a semi-divine nature. For Arius, the Son was not fully God, but only like God. Further, for Arius, the Son was not even really a "son." He wasn't born of the Father, but was created by the Father.

The problem with this view was that if the Son was not fully divine, then the Son cannot fully reveal God to us, nor can He fully bring us back to God. Because God is infinitely perfect, anything that isn't God is necessarily an infinite distance from God. Arius's view would mean that the ladder between God and humanity does not extend all the way to the top.

So it is clear that this view has theological problems. It still leaves us separated from God. And it has another huge problem.

The view that Jesus is only *like* God does not fit with Scripture.

- Scripture tells us that Jesus reveals the Father (John 14:8–9).
- Scripture tells us that Jesus and the Father are one (John 10:30).
- Scripture tells us that Jesus is born of God (or begotten), not created (John 3:16).
- Scripture also tells us that Jesus is *called* God (John 20:28)!

When the problems with Arius's ideas became clear, the church ruled at the Council of Nicea (in AD 325) that we cannot talk about the Son as merely being *like* God, or being a "creation" of God, we must declare Jesus to *be* God.

We hear, then, in this part of the Nicene Creed (the whole of which is still recited weekly in many churches), the church's rejection of Arius's view that Jesus is only semi-divine:

We believe in one Lord, Jesus Christ,
the only Son of God,
eternally *begotten* of the Father,
God from God, Light from Light,
True God from *true God,*
begotten, not made,
of one being with the Father . . .

To return to the central analogy of this unit, because Jesus is *true God*, we know that the ladder goes all the way to the top.

One of the great theologians of the church, St. Athanasius, uses a powerful analogy to describe the incarnation. In coming all the way down to earth, the Son honors humanity by His presence in the way that a king honors a city by coming to live there:

> And now the very corruption of death no longer holds ground against human beings because of the indwelling Word. . . . As when a great king has entered some large city and made his dwelling in one of the houses in it, such a city is certainly made worthy of high honor, and no longer does any enemy or bandit descend upon it, but it is rather reckoned worthy of all care because of the king's having taken residence in one of the houses; so also does it happen with the King of all. Coming himself into our realm, and dwelling in a body like the others, every design of the enemy against human beings has henceforth ceased, and the corruption of death, which had prevailed formerly against them, perished. (Athanasius, *On the Incarnation* [Yonkers, NY: St. Vladimir's, 2011], 58)

When Jesus came down to our level and became, as one wit charmingly put it, "God in the bod," great honor was bestowed on humanity.

It's a bit like going on vacation and seeing a famous celebrity staying at the same resort. When that happens, many of the other vacationers will suddenly see the resort as an even more luxurious place.

But there's more to it than that, as Athanasius says. Now that the Son has become a man, all humans can be protected by the power of the King who is with us. Eugene Peterson, in *The Message*, translates John 1:14 like this: "The Word became flesh and blood, and moved into the neighborhood."

In this sense, it's like having a police officer move in next door. We know that the presence of the police car on the street will ward off criminals. With Jesus living next to us we can know that no enemy, not even the last, great enemy of death, can ever truly harm us.

In a very famous passage in Christian theology, Gregory of Nazianzus, a fourth-century bishop, argues that it is absolutely necessary that the Son takes on the whole of human nature in order to save us.

Arguing against a heresy called Apollinarianism, which said that Jesus Christ did not have a human mind, Gregory made an important point that has guided Christian thinking ever since. "The unassumed is the unhealed," Gregory declared, "but what is united with God is also being saved" (St. Gregory of Nazianzus, *On God and Christ* [Yonkers, NY: St. Vladimir's, 2002], 158).

The main point here is that the Son had to be united Himself to a *fully* human nature in order to repair the damage of fallen humanity. Because our whole person is fallen, mind and body, Jesus Christ must become fully like us: a true human.

The Apollinarian view, that Jesus Christ did not have a human mind, would be something like what we do when we control a video game character. The divine Son would merely be directing what looked and acted like a human, but would not really be a human.

Gregory goes on to make his case in powerful words about why Jesus Christ cannot merely be God using a human body like a puppet:

> Had half of Adam fallen, what was assumed and is being saved [by the Son] would have been half too; but if the whole fell he is united to the whole of what was born and being saved wholly. [The Apollinarians then] are not to begrudge us our entire salvation or to fit out a Savior with only bones and sinews and the picture of a human being. (Ibid.)

This insight, that Jesus Christ is fully divine and fully human, has an additional implication. It means that when we look at Jesus, we not only see what God looks like, but what humanity is supposed to look like as well. Jesus teaches us what it means to be God, but also what it means to be human: hungry, emotional, sleepy; but also holy and joyful.

5 The clearest statement of the church's understanding of the two natures is from the fifth century, and is found in the Creed of Chalcedon. In an attempt to clarify for everyone what the Scripture shows us about Jesus, the creed defines for us how to speak about the incarnate Son: one person with two natures.

Here is the creed, in full:

> We, then, following the holy Fathers, all with one consent, teach men to
> confess one and the same Son, our Lord Jesus Christ, the same perfect
> in Godhead and also perfect in manhood; truly God and truly man, of
> a reasonable soul and body; consubstantial with us according to the
> manhood; in all things like unto us, without sin; begotten before all ages
> of the Father according to the Godhead, and in these latter days, for us and
> for our salvation, born of the virgin Mary, the mother of God, according
> to the manhood; one and the same Christ, Son, Lord, Only-begotten,
> to be acknowledged in two natures, *without confusion, without change,*
> *without division, without separation*; the distinction of natures being by no
> means taken away by the union, but rather the property of each nature
> being preserved, and concurring in one Person and one Subsistence, not
> parted or divided into two persons, but one and the same Son, and only
> begotten, God the Word, the Lord Jesus Christ, as the prophets from
> the beginning have declared concerning him, and the Lord Jesus Christ
> himself taught us, and the Creed of the holy Fathers has handed down to
> us. [I have altered some of the wording (*italicized*) here to make it clearer
> to modern readers.]

UNIT 3 / QUESTION 6:
WHY DID THE SON OF GOD BECOME HUMAN?

Thomas Oden discusses God's motivation when he writes, "Redemptive love
is ... the primordial purpose and motivation preceding creation. Its manifes-
tation is the reason God creates" (*Classic Christianity: A Systematic Theology* [New
York, NY: Harper Collins, 1992], 529).

Oden's point here is significant. Like parents who adopt a special-needs child
knowing all the challenges ahead, God creates, knowing full well that the tree of
the cross will follow after the Tree of the Knowledge of Good and Evil.

The Father knows that Jesus will have to be sent after Adam.

The Father knows the pain and suffering that await the older Son, when He is sent to recover the younger son.

Redemptive love was God's motivation from the beginning. And this never changed. This motivation to love was not naive love on God's part. God's love always bore on its back the scars of the whip.

Peter Abelard, a medieval theologian, focused on the way that God's love, when understood, accomplishes God's redemptive purpose. When we look at Jesus we see God's love for us most clearly. For Abelard, this love changes us, transforming us into lovers of God and others:

> Love is increased by the faith which we have concerning Christ because, on account of the belief that God in Christ has united our human nature to himself, and by suffering in that same nature has demonstrated to us that supreme love of which Christ himself speaks: "Greater love has no one than this" (John 15:13). We are thus joined through his grace to him and our neighbor by an unbreakable bond of love. . . . Therefore, our redemption through the suffering of Christ is that deeper love within us which not only frees us from slavery to sin, but also secures for us the true liberty of the children of God, in order that we might do all things out of love rather than out of fear—love for him who has shown us such grace that no greater can be found. (cited in Alister McGrath, *The Christian Theology Reader* [Oxford: Wiley-Blackwell, 2001], 299-300)

Though this passage leaves out the *other* ways that God's action in Christ redeems us, it does get one thing thunderingly right: God's love is fundamentally *redemptive*.

God's love is not merely an enabling love, which merely helps us to get out of our problems (like a parent who bails his children out of tough spots but then leaves them to do it again). God's love is a redeeming love. When we experience the true nature of God's love, we are *transformed*.

 Moving from discussing God's *motivation* to God's *goal*, I have skipped over an important step, God's *means* for accomplishing His goal: the incarnation, death, resurrection, and ascension of Jesus. I'll talk about God's means in the next two lessons, but I want it to be clear that God's goal is not something that could be accomplished easily. It *costs*.

 God's goal of making us family ties into the discussion in Unit 5 of the pattern of redemption.

God's covenant with Abraham in the Old Testament established a new family, a nation of people.

God's covenant with Moses established the rules of God's household, a distinct way of being in the world as God's holy nation.

God's covenant with David established a clear head to the household, a king to rule over them.

This is the pattern, but the covenants were not complete in accomplishing God's goal of making a family.

They were good, but imperfect. In fact, in Galatians 4, Paul compares the law given through Moses to a form of slavery, because the Israelites were in a state of child-likeness: subject (as a child is) to teachers and nannies. The covenants established a family of God on earth, but did not bring the people of Israel into a state of full sonship.

Paul wrote,

> Before the coming of this faith [in Christ], we were held in custody under the law, locked up until the faith that was to come would be revealed. So the law was our guardian until Christ came that we might be justified by faith. Now that this faith has come, we are no longer under a guardian. . . . What I am saying is that as long as an heir is underage, he is no different from a slave, although he owns the whole estate. The heir is subject to guardians and trustees until the time set by his father. (Gal. 3:23–24; 4:1–2)

Now that Jesus has come, the situation is different. We have reached "adulthood" through Christ and have the status of fully grown children.

> But when the set time had fully come, God sent his Son, born of a woman, born under the law, to redeem those under the law, that we might receive adoption to sonship. Because you are his sons, God sent the Spirit of his Son into our hearts, the Spirit who calls out, "*Abba*, Father." So you are no longer a slave, but God's child; and since you are his child, God has made you also an heir. (Gal. 4:4–7)

In coming to fulfill the previous covenants, Jesus fulfills all of them and establishes a new way of being family.

Jesus is like David, Moses, and Abraham, but more. Jesus rules over His people as the perfect King. He empowers them for holiness through the Spirit. And He offers blessing to all the peoples of the earth. But under the new covenant, we are a true family, experiencing the intimacy and responsibilities of mature children.

This is a bold statement, but I think a true one: *everything in the entire Bible is pointed toward this goal, to bring God's people again into the family of God.*

The offer to be God's people is not just aimed at one set of people, living in a particular place, with a particular family line, but *all* people. God's offer to be family is now open to all. As Jesus said to His disciples, "My Father's house has many rooms" (John 14:2).

There are beds made for us all. The door is unlocked. Jesus is waiting up for us. The light on the front porch is on, no matter how late it gets.

UNIT 4 / QUESTION 7: WHAT IS SALVATION?

 The church has always understood the work that Jesus did on the cross in two main ways. The first is that Jesus solves the rupture between *God and us*. He bears the punishment for sin, or, in slightly different language, Jesus "pays the debt" we owed to God.

St. Anselm, a medieval theologian and bishop we've discussed before, wrote about this in his book, *Why God Became Man*. Anselm points out the humans are the ones who owe a debt to God, but are unable to pay the debt. The debt was incurred by our sin. But there's nothing we can do to repay the debt. Even living righteous, sinless lives (if this were possible) will not pay for previous sins, because we always owe perfect obedience to God. Fulfilling our duties *now* will not pay for debts in the past.

Think about it like this. Let's say that you fall behind on your rent, but only make enough money to pay the rent for this month, not the last month's. You couldn't very well settle things with your landlord by offering to pay the rent in the future, because that doesn't cover the payment for missed rent in the past. You feel bad about this, and wonder what can be done to make it up to the landlord. But there's nothing you can do. He can simply forgive the debt, but then he's out the money you owe him.

In this case, we *ought* to make it up the landlord, but *can't*. The landlord can forgive the debt, but that won't repair the breach between you. (Recall as well the analogy of the Thanksgiving dinner I used in this lesson.) There's a problem.

But let's say you hear a knock at the door, and it's your sister, who wants to move in and be your roommate. You explain the situation and she agrees to move in and pay the debt for you. In this way the debt is repaid on your behalf and the relationship with the landlord is repaired.

Jesus comes down to earth and becomes human (our roommate). He lives with us in the same apartment and pays the debt on our behalf to his Father (the landlord).

Anselm explains it like this:

> [There is a saving work that needs to be done. But,] God will not do it, because he has no debt to pay; and man will not do it, because he cannot. Therefore, in order that the God-man may perform this, it is necessary

that the same being should be perfect God and perfect man, in order to make this atonement. For he cannot and ought not to do it, unless he be very God and very man (Anselm, "Cur Deus Homo" in *St. Anselm* [Lasalle: Open Court: 1968], 246).

It is important to understand that the 'debt' we owed to God was a) very large, and b) one that requires *punishment*. This is why many theologians have talked about the necessity of the cross in repaying the debt to God. It is not simply that Jesus had to die, but that He bear our punishment. In this sense we can think about our sin as a crime. Jesus' crucifixion alongside criminals is important. He takes our place in the divine law-court, taking the full sentence of the just judge (the Father).

Crucifixion was the Roman punishment for rebels, people who fought against Roman rule. The Romans thought they were protecting their earthly authority by passing sentence on Jesus, but God used this as a way of putting the punishment for all humanity on Jesus. Lifted high on a cross, Jesus takes our punishment as *rebels* against God (Romans 5:10–11).

No human could have paid the debt of punishment for all humanity, because we were already under the sentence of death. But Jesus did not owe this debt to God. This is why only the God-man Jesus could pay the debt on our behalf (1 John 2:2; Hebrews 9:22).

2 A second key way of understanding what Jesus did for us in His death and resurrection is that Jesus rescued us from captivity to death and the devil. Where the satisfaction theory of salvation resolves the problem between God and us, the "rescue" theory resolves our danger at the hands of the devil and the enemy of death.

After the fall, we were trapped in bondage to death and the powers of evil. We were caught in the irresistible pull of *hell*, which tugged on us with the force of a black hole's gravity. There was no escape.

But the Father did something we might almost say was "tricky." We were in bondage to hell, but He offered Jesus as a ransom.

An ancient theologian named Rufinus of Aquileia captures this idea by using the analogy of Christ as a kind of worm on a fishhook.

> [The purpose of the incarnation] was that the divine virtue of the Son of God might be like a kind of hook hidden beneath the form of human flesh ... to lure on the prince of this world [Satan] to a contest; that the Son might offer him his human flesh as a bait and that the divinity which lay underneath might catch him and hold him fast with its hook ... Then, just as a fish when it seizes a baited hook not only fails to drag off the bait but is itself dragged out of the water to serve as food for others; so he that had the power of death seized the body of Jesus in death, unaware of the hook of divinity which lay hidden inside. Having swallowed it, [Satan] was immediately caught. The gates of hell were broken, and he was, as it were drawn up from the pit (Alister McGrath, *The Christian Theology Reader*, 4th ed. [Oxford: Wiley-Blackwell, 2011], 292).

This is a powerful and charming image, though one that should not be pressed too far. God is not deceptive, merely far more clever than all earthly powers. But it helps to capture the dramatic nature of the resurrection: the ultimate plot twist.

Killing Jesus might have *seemed* to be Satan's ultimate defeat of God's plan. It certainly seemed to be the end of the story to Jesus' disciples. But it wasn't the end of the story. Instead, God defeated the power of death and the devil though Jesus' death and resurrection. Jesus went down to hell, but then broke out again, shattering the locked doors.

This theme of "ransom" is clearly taught in scripture. In Mark 10:45, we hear Jesus speaking about Himself as one who comes to offer His life as a trade: "the Son of Man did not come to be served, but to serve, and to give His life as a ransom for many."

And in Colossians 2:13-15, we hear both themes, *reconciliation* and *ransom*, tied together:

When you were dead in your sins and in the uncircumcision of your sinful nature, God made you alive with Christ. He forgave us all our sins, having canceled the written code, with its regulations, that was against us and that stood opposed to us; he took it away, nailing it to the cross. And having disarmed the powers and authorities, he made a public spectacle of them, triumphing over them by the cross.

It is important to keep in mind that Jesus does not merely offer us forgiveness for sin, but also offers us triumph over death and the devil. This is the good news, a front page headline that never ceases to be true, declaring victory over sin *and* death.

UNIT 4 / QUESTION 8:
WHAT IS REQUIRED FOR SALVATION?

The Greek word for "repent" is *metanoia*, which means "a change of mind." It is derived from *meta* (meaning "after" or "change after") and *nous* (meaning "mind"). To repent implies a change from one way of being to another, as when Jesus said in Luke 5:32, "I have not come to call the righteous, but sinners to repentance."

"Faith," in Greek, is *pistis*, which implies a deep trust. This belief is not merely head knowledge, but a commitment to follow through on this knowledge. Many times when Jesus speaks of someone's faith, He is not merely talking about something they think is true, but the way that this conviction leads them to action. For instance, in Mark 2, some friends of a paralyzed man cut a hole in a roof to get their friend to Jesus, the crowds being too difficult to push through. Jesus "sees their faith." He sees the way that they trust that He has the power to heal and take extreme action based on that belief.

The comparison of the repentance of a sinner and the repentance of a rebel is not an accidental one. In Mark 1:15, when Jesus announces the kingdom of God, He speaks with full authority of a returning king, coming back to a land that is rightfully His.

N. T. Wright pointed out that this call to repentance by Jesus was, at the time of His speaking it, a specific call to His people Israel to join God's plan to redeem the world.

The people of Israel are not just called upon to amend their lives, but to abandon any other agendas they may have, and get on board with Jesus' mission. This call to repentance is as much *political* as it is *moral* or *spiritual*. It is not just about aligning our lives with God's rules, but about aligning our lives with God's specific plans: what God is doing in Jesus Christ.

It is for this reason that we hear Jesus condemning those cities where His miracles were done, but where people would not "repent" (Luke 10:13). It is not merely that Jesus wanted them to stop sinning, but to join in His mission of reestablishing God's kingdom. Israel was failing to join in with God's plan to redeem Israel and through Israel, the entire world. Hence, Wright writes, "'Repentance' in Jesus' context, then, would have carried the connotations of 'what Israel must do if YHWH is to restore her fortunes at last'" (N. T. Wright, *Jesus and the Victory of God: Christian Origins and The Question Of God*, vol. 2 [London: Fortress Press, 1997], ch. 7, section 2.1).

To put this in the form of an analogy, imagine that the publisher of a newspaper walked out into the bullpen, where all the journalists are, and shouted, "Stop the presses! Something huge has just happened!" Yet many of the journalists kept on writing the stories they were assigned and ignored the publisher. Even if these journalists were carrying out their previous assignments properly, they aren't getting on board with the publisher's plan.

Keeping in mind this larger sense of repentance, then, we can see that it isn't enough to follow all the rules. We need to follow the right person. Since we often get off track and pursue our own designs, God may call us to "change our minds" if we get off track from the plan He has for us. If we refuse, no matter how good the things we are doing might be, we're in rebellion against Him.

 It's important to keep in mind that the "godly sorrow" the Bible talks about is different than despair. To despair is to give up all hope, and this itself is a sin.

As Paul says in 2 Corinthians 7:10, "Godly sorrow brings repentance that leads to salvation and leaves no regret, but worldly sorrow brings death."

When we experience godly sorrow we are truly sad for our sin, but there is a silver lining of joy, knowing that God is ready and willing to save us. Jonathan Edwards describes repentance as a kind of "pleasure." Because we know that forgiveness is ready at hand, it is a "sweet sorrow" (Jonathan Edwards, "The Pleasantness of Religion").

This sweet sorrow for sin is one of the reasons for the strange quality to Christian testimonies. Though Christians often talk about our sin when we share our stories of salvation, there is a kind of pleasure in hearing about the ways that God has delivered and forgiven us. True repentance leaves no regret.

4 Frederick Buechner, *Telling the Truth: The Gospel as Tragedy, Comedy, and Fairy Tale* (San Francisco, CA: HarperSanFrancisco, 1977), 7.

5 A very helpful distinction, when it comes to belief, is between believing *that* there is a God, and believing *in* God. Both are necessary for true faith. But they aren't the same thing.

To fully trust in God we have to believe with our *intellect*. As C. S. Lewis says, "I am not asking anyone to accept Christianity if his best reasoning tells him that the weight of the evidence is against it. That is not the point at which Faith comes in" (C. S. Lewis, *Mere Christianity*, 140).

Believing that there is a God is a key ingredient in faith. And there are many good reasons for believing there is a God. There are arguments for God's existence from reason. There are arguments for the historicity of Jesus and His resurrection. And there is the evidence of the presence of God in the lives of believers.

In order for some people to come to a point of having saving faith, they must first come to understand the evidence for God's existence and the truthfulness of the Bible. Once they do, they will have the knowledge that God exists and offers salvation to them.

But believing there is a God is not the same as trusting *in* God. As James writes, even demons believe in God, and "shudder" (James 2:19).

It is possible to believe God exists yet not want to have anything to do with Him.

The kind of faith that saves us requires *personal trust*. It requires a commitment.

We hear this in Jesus' words to Martha before the resurrection of Lazarus, "I am the resurrection and the life. The one who believes in me will live, even though they die" (John 11:25).

Now, this might sound like a neat, two-step process. First intellectual understanding, then personal trust. But things are rarely as tidy as this. Very often in life we only have some degree of intellectual confidence, which we must act on. But in the doing, we discover more good reasons to believe. As we follow Jesus in trust, very often our intellectual understanding grows. To put it in the terms I've been using, believing in God leads us to greater certainty *that* God is there and His words are true.

Once again, N. T. Wright's work is helpful here to fully understand the way that repenting and believing are not just about a change of heart and life, but are also about a change of *loyalty*. As Wright points out in *Jesus and the Victory of God*, the phrase that Jesus uses, "repent and believe," had a political (or almost military) dimension.

In the same century that Jesus lived, and the gospel of Mark was written, a Roman political advisor named Josephus records his attempts to stop a rebel group that was fighting against Rome. The leader of the rebels tried to have Josephus killed, but was unsuccessful. So Josephus traveled to where the rebels were hiding and encountered them with a mighty military force. Surrounded and outgunned, Josephus called for the rebel leader and told him

> that "I was not a stranger to that treacherous design he had against me . . . however, I would forgive him what he had done already, if he would repent of it, and be faithful to me hereafter." And thus, upon his promise to do all that I desired, I let him go. (*The Life of Flavius Josephus*, §110–11)

As Wright points out, the specific words Josephus uses to call the rebels to surrender could just as easily have been translated "repent and believe in me" (*metanoesein kai pistos*) (Wright, *Jesus and the Victory of God*, ch. 7, section 2.1).

Even though they have tried to kill Josephus, the rebels are forgiven, if they will repent and be loyal.

Having this in our minds, the words of Jesus in Mark 1:15 resound even more loudly. Jesus is not merely calling people to stop sinning (though He is doing that too). He is calling them to declare their true allegiance to the kingdom of God.

UNIT 5 / QUESTION 9:
WHAT ARE THE BENEFITS OF SALVATION?

The term Paul uses to describe the way we have peace with God is "justification" (Romans 5:1). This is the main theological label to describe the beginning of our redemption. The term can be somewhat confusing because we might be led to think that by "justification" we are actually made to be just (or righteous) people. And though some theologians have understood justification in this way, there is a better, more biblical way of thinking about it.

As N. T. Wright explains in *Justification: God's Plan & Paul's Vision*, when Paul uses the term, he is drawing on Old Testament sources, which imply the conferring of a legal status, not a moral one. A legal framework is helpful to get our heads around the distinction.

Imagine being in a court, accused of a crime. But instead of being found guilty, we are declared innocent (or not guilty). The judge is not saying that you are a good person, but that you will not be convicted of the crime.

Wright writes this about the biblical term "to justify" (*dikaioo*):

> [To justify] does not denote *an action which transforms someone* so much as a *declaration which grants them a status*. It is the *status* of the person which is transformed by the action of "justification," not the *character*.

It is in this sense that "justification" "makes" someone "righteous," just as the officiant at a wedding service might be said to "make" the couple husband and wife—a change of status, accompanied (it is hoped) by a steady transformation of the heart, but a real change of status even if both parties are entering the union out of pure convenience. (N. T. Wright, *Justification: God's Plan & Paul's Vision* [Downers Grove, IL: InterVarsity Press, 2009], 91)

To return to the example we have been discussing in this section, justification is a "pardon." A pardon is a legal action authorities can perform. A president, or a judge, has the power to legally pardon someone for their crimes, meaning they cannot be punished for them. They are cleared in the eyes of the law.

This is how John Wesley understood the meaning of justification. Justification is primarily to be understood as *pardon*.

In his sermon "Justification by Faith," Wesley points out that justification is not "being made actually just and righteous. This is *sanctification*; which is in some degree the immediate *fruit* of justification, but nevertheless is a distinct gift from God."

To make things a little plainer, justification is something that God does *for us* (through Jesus' atoning sacrifice on our behalf), while regeneration and sanctification are things God does *in us* (through the work of the Spirit). Justification sets us at peace again with God, but doesn't change our inner reality. Regeneration and sanctification begin to happen in us immediately upon justification, but they aren't the same thing.

All this might seem to be unnecessary hair-splitting, but it is important to try, as much as possible, to hear the words of Scripture clearly. When terms get muddled, bad ideas about God inevitably follow.

One bad idea that follows from an incorrect view of justification (the view that justification "makes" us just or righteous people) is related to the fact that, when we are saved, we still have lots of sinful desires and habits. Our characters haven't fully changed. If we hold an incorrect idea of justification and therefore believe that God has made us just or righteous, but yet we know that we aren't this way, confusion results. Sometimes Christians have come to believe that God somehow now believes us to be fully righteous. He *sees* us as righteous. But if we aren't this way, we have to assume that God is somehow deceiving Himself, which would mean that God believes something that isn't true. This is a problem. It means that God knows less about our sin than we do ourselves. Which can't be true.

A proper view of justification as pardon clears away all these problems. God has not forgotten that we were sinners any more than the king in the example has forgotten that his new soldiers were once rebels. God remembers these things. God treats us differently because He has forgiven us. Likewise, God is not deceived about those sinful desires and habits that remain in us. He sees these faults and works with us to change them.

One of the reasons this idea can be so hard to accept is that we're bad at fully forgiving people. We remember the sins of others and sometimes still hold little scraps of resentment in our hearts. I think this is why, in Isaiah 43:25, God says that He will "remember our sins no more." God is speaking metaphorically here to communicate to fallen people how good He is at forgiving. When God forgives, it is *as if* God has amnesia about our sins. God has to accommodate to our level of understanding to communicate His perfect forgiveness. God doesn't really forget, but God does fully forgive.

Being given new life is an important element of salvation, but it is sometimes forgotten. As we saw in the example of the rebels, they were not only under the threat of punishment from the king, they were also starving to death, shivering from cold out in the elements. It is not enough to save the rebels simply by forgiving them. If left alone, they will die out in the wilderness.

This relates to our condition because, after the fall, we humans were destined to destruction if we remained apart from God (Romans 6:23). We didn't have what we needed in ourselves to maintain our physical life, or our spiritual life. We were dead, inside and outside.

Ephesians 2:1–3 says this clearly:

As for you, you were dead in your transgressions and sins, in which you used to live when you followed the ways of this world and of the ruler of the kingdom of the air, the spirit who is now at work in those who are disobedient. All of us also lived among them at one time, gratifying the cravings of our flesh and following its desires and thoughts. Like the rest, we were by nature deserving of wrath.

Being dead means that we had no power to live rightly. As Paul shows in the verse above, apart from God we are under the power of sin and the devil (the ruler of the kingdom of the air). If we were merely forgiven, we still couldn't serve God because we were still dead in sin.

Regeneration (or being "given new life") solves this problem. Being "made alive in Christ" brings us back from the dead with Jesus' resurrection power (Eph. 2:5). This is why Jesus talks about being "born again" (John 3:3). And Paul talks about being "new creations" in Christ (2 Cor. 5:17).

The phrases like "born again" and "new creation" are charged with biblical meaning. They bring us right back to the garden of Eden, when God made humans for the first time. It is worth remembering that Jesus' resurrection is discovered "on the first day of the week" (Mark 16:9). Any faithful Jew reading these words would immediately be reminded of the first day of creation from Genesis 1.

With the resurrection, Jesus has "rebooted" God's purpose in creation. He has made it possible to have the kind of life and love that was in the garden again.

One last thing is important to mention here. Though justification (pardon) and regeneration (new life) are distinct works of God in Christ, regeneration happens in us at the same time as justification. It happens when we repent and believe, but it adds another element to our salvation.

We might think about it like this:

Justification saves us from the *penalty* of sin. Regeneration saves us from the *power* of sin.

Both actions of God begin when we repent and believe. And all this is made possible by Jesus.

Jesus' death offers us the chance to be forgiven. Jesus' resurrection offers us the chance to be new creations.

 John Wesley uses this famous analogy in "The Principles of a Methodist Farther Explained":

> Our main doctrines, which include all the rest, are three—that of repentance, of faith, and of holiness. The first of these we account, as it were, the porch of religion; the next, the door; the third, religion itself.

Though I will talk more about the differences between the stages of salvation in the next lesson, it is helpful to hear from Wesley about what he means by these terms: repentance, faith, and holiness.

Here are some further quotes from the same source:

> [REPENTANCE:] That *repentance*, or conviction of sin, which is always previous to faith (either in a higher or lower degree, as it pleases God), we describe in words to this effect: "When men feel in themselves the heavy burden of sin, see damnation to be the reward of it, behold with the eye of their mind the horror of hell; they tremble, they quake, and are inwardly touched with sorrowfulness of heart . . ."

> [JUSTIFYING FAITH:] "The right and true Christian *faith* is, not only to believe that the Holy Scriptures and the articles of our faith are true, but also to have a sure trust and confidence to be saved from everlasting damnation, through Christ." Perhaps it may be expressed more clearly thus: "A sure trust and confidence which a man hath in God, that by the merits of Christ his sins are *forgiven*, and he reconciled to the favor of God."

> [HOLINESS or SANCTIFICATION:] Religion itself (I choose to use the very words wherein I described it long ago) we define, "The loving

God with all our heart, and our neighbor as ourselves; and in that love *abstaining from all evil, and doing all possible good to all men."* . . . Religion we conceive to be no other than love; the love of God and of all mankind; the loving God 'with all our heart, and soul, and strength,' as having 'first loved us,' as the fountain of all the good we have received, and of all we ever hope to enjoy; and the loving every soul which God hath made, every man on earth, as our own soul. . . . This love we believe to be the medicine of life, the never-failing remedy for all the evils of a disordered world, for all the miseries and vices of men. Wherever this is, there are virtue and happiness going hand in hand. There is humbleness of mind, gentleness, longsuffering, the whole *image of God*, and, at the same time, a peace that passeth all understanding, and joy unspeakable and full of glory. [*Emphasis mine.*]

Wesley here does not discuss "new birth," but he hasn't forgotten it. In the note on "new life" in this lesson I discuss Wesley's understanding of the term, and how it always accompanies justification (or "pardon").

 I'll talk about these new ways of living in the next lesson, using the term "sanctification."

UNIT 5 / QUESTION 10: WHAT HAPPENS WHEN WE LIVE OUT OUR SALVATION IN CHRIST?

In talking about sanctification (or holiness/righteousness), it's important to keep in mind what the goal or purpose is. Though it is easy to talk about sanctification as simply being without sin (not breaking any of God's laws), this is merely a *negative* account of what it means.

In a *positive* sense, sanctification is simply being able to fulfill the law given to us by Jesus.

And this law is to "love the Lord your God with all your heart and with all your soul and with all your mind and with all your strength," and to "love your neighbor as yourself" (Mark 12:30-31).

And this law is beautiful.

Sanctification doesn't just *take something away*. It *gives something better*. It gives the ability to do what we've always wanted deep down. To be connected to the most perfect being imaginable. And to love and care for our fellow humans. The end result is perfect joy.

Our problem, very often, is that we don't really *trust that* God wants the best for us. We think that if we follow Jesus completely we won't be happy. So we hold on to sins, big and small. Even though we know they're not good for us, they're better than what we can imagine. We're like children who refuse to try new and delicious foods at a 5-star restaurant, asking instead for chicken strips and french fries.

When it comes to sanctification, we're excited by the idea of getting rid of some bad habits that are making us miserable, and we like the idea of being more loving to others, but we haven't gotten excited about the idea of really, truly becoming like Jesus.

We don't just have fallen bodies and souls, we also have fallen *imaginations*.

We can't imagine what it would be like to really be like Jesus. And when we do imagine being made holy, the idea can sometimes seem a little boring. We sort of understand that sin hurts us. But we understand the way that holiness helps us even less.

Very often, when we think about sanctification, we think about it as being a little better version of ourselves. Almost completely the same, but with a few updates and improvements. C. S. Lewis captures this failure of imagination well in *Mere Christianity*. He writes,

> Imagine yourself as a living house. God comes in to rebuild that house. At first, perhaps, you can understand what He is doing. He is getting the drains right and stopping the leaks in the roof and so on: you knew that those jobs needed doing and so you are not surprised. But presently He starts knocking the house about in a way that hurts abominably and does not seem to make any sense. What on earth is He up to? The explanation is

111

that He is building quite a different house from the one you thought of—throwing out a new wing here, putting on an extra floor there, running up towers, making courtyards. You thought you were being made into a decent little cottage: but He is building a palace. He intends to come and live in it Himself. (C. S. Lewis, *Mere Christianity*, 205)

 The New Testament Greek word for sanctification is *hagiasmos*, which means "holiness." It shares a root with the word for "saint" (*hagios*), or "holy ones."

The idea that sanctification is a process is at once helpful and also a little misleading. It *is* a process, and normally takes quite a lot of time. Like a baby newly born, we have to grow into the likeness of Christ (2 Peter 3:18).

But it is not a *natural* process. As with justification, sanctification requires as much grace from God as the very first work He did in us. We depend on God to empower us to remove sin from our lives, to love our neighbors fully, and to love God with all our being (Mark 12:29–31).

This does not mean, however, that we do not play any part in the process. Our cooperation is needed.

As with justification, God's grace requires a response from us. We can *resist* the grace of salvation. And if we pull against God long and hard, God will let us win the tug-o-war in the end. John Wesley wrote:

> God worketh in you; therefore you can work: otherwise it would be impossible. If he did not work it would be impossible for you to work out your own salvation. . . . Secondly, God worketh in you; therefore you must work: you must be "workers together with him" (they are the very words of the Apostle), otherwise he will cease working. ("On Working Out Our Own Salvation")

So the process of sanctification requires cooperation. God's work enables us to work with Him. But we must work at it.

Sanctification is also not *ultimately* a gradual process. When *we* try and clean something, we know that it is never fully clean. Just *mostly* clean. By clean we really mean "clean enough."

God's grace isn't like this. It's not a vacuum that's sucking up all the bits of sin, but still leaving particles too small to pull up, or dirty corners where the vacuum can't reach. God is all-powerful, and if we let Him, He can eventually remove all the final bits. In the same way that through justification we were able to "leap" from guilty to innocent, so too with sanctification we are able to leap from "mostly holy" to "entirely holy" (cf. John Wesley, "The Repentance of Believers").

 C. S. Lewis, *The Problem of Pain*, 29–30.

 The word "perfection" can be a stumbling block for many of us, because we often say things like, "Nobody's perfect!" And we know that even the holiest person you meet doesn't know everything, and even makes mistakes in judgment from time to time. This is why John Wesley was clear, when he wrote on perfection (the end goal of sanctification), to say what perfection is not, as well as what it is. Wesley writes,

> Christian perfection, therefore, does not imply (as some men seem to have imagined) an exemption either from ignorance or mistake, or infirmities or temptations" (John Wesley, "Christian Perfection"). Even as we are being made holy, the weakness and limitation of our human nature remains. Deliverance from sin does not mean that we know all things, or that we have perfect judgment about what to do in every situation. We still have bodily and mental weakness, and can even still be tempted. Sanctification removes sin from our lives, but we will still be prone to error, mistakes, and temptation until God completes the act of salvation by glorifying our resurrected selves.

There is a final step in the process of salvation, which is called "glorification." I'll talk about this in chapter 15.

UNIT 6 / QUESTION 11:
WHO IS THE HOLY SPIRIT?

In the life of the early church, the official theology of the Holy Spirit developed more slowly than the theology of the Son. At the first Council of Nicea in AD 325, the official creed of the church merely mentioned that we believe "in the Holy Spirit." It was quickly seen that this was not enough, and in AD 381, at the Council of Constantinople, the church said more about the Spirit's role:

> We believe in the Holy Spirit, the Lord, the Giver of Life,
> who proceeds from the Father,
> who with the Father and the Son
> is worshiped and glorified,
> who has spoken through the prophets.

This language was adopted into the original Nicene Creed, and is used all over the world today.

A further development happened in theology at the 11th Council of Toledo, when the Western church clarified that the Spirit also proceeds from the Son. This addition, known as the "Filioque clause," has become part of the confession of the Nicene Creed in most Roman Catholic and Protestant traditions.

It is worth noting that the Eastern and Western creeds are not contradictory. The original version of the creed *does not* say that the Spirit does not proceed from the Son as well. The Western version merely says more than the original creed does.

Nevertheless, the addition of this wording played a part in the division between Eastern and Western churches, which has continued to the time of this writing.

Though there is always tragedy in the division of the church, the acknowledgment that the Spirit also proceeds from the Son has much scriptural weight.

For instance, the Spirit is referred to as *both* the Spirit of the Father (Matthew 10:20) and the Spirit of the Son (Romans 8:9).

Furthermore, in the action of the Trinity in the world, Jesus *sends* the Spirit (John 14:16; 15:26).

This might seem to resolve the issue, but the story is much more complicated than that, because we also see in Scripture that the Spirit *sends* the Son in the sense that it is by the Spirit that Jesus is begotten of the Virgin Mary and empowered for ministry (Matthew 1:18; Luke 4:1).

If the action of the Trinity in the world is our best guide to understanding the inner life of the Trinity itself, then perhaps an even more nuanced way of speaking of the relations of the persons is called for. Some theologians (like Tom Smail) have suggested a better way of speaking of the relation of the triune persons: *the Son is begotten by the Father through the Spirit, and the Spirit proceeds from the Father through the Son* (Thomas Smail, "The Holy Spirit in the Holy Trinity," in *Nicene Christianity*, ed. Christopher Seitz [Grand Rapids, MI: Brazos, 2001].)

That the witness of Scripture shows a more dynamic relationship between the persons of the Trinity than the formal language of the creed allows should be no surprise. The creeds are meant to offer a clear and simple way of speaking about God that is less nuanced than the reality itself. This does not mean that it is inaccurate.

In the same way that a roadmap is simpler than the streets it portrays, the creeds offer us a true-but-simplified picture of God.

It is true to say that the Spirit proceeds from the Father and the Son. But the reality is more detailed. Even more detailed, in fact, than the picture that Scripture gives us. The reality of God is bigger than our human words and human minds can comprehend.

The push and pull between the East and West over the way we speak about the Spirit, and the complex picture that Scripture paints, should not make us worry that our theology is false, but simply that our theology is only a sketch of a high-definition reality.

As I've said before, the truest story we can tell about the world is the story of the Trinity's action in it. Looking back, we can see the triune persons at work from the very beginning. But this is only in *hindsight*. In the unfolding of the story of Scripture, the persons of the Trinity were revealed more gradually.

As Gregory of Nazianzus wrote, "The Old Testament preached the Father openly and the Son more obscurely. The New Testament revealed the Son, and hinted at the divinity of the Holy Spirit. Now the Spirit dwells in us, and is revealed more clearly to us" (St. Gregory of Nazianzus, *On God and Christ* [Yonkers, NY: St. Vladimir's, 2002], Oration 31.26).

To put this in different terms: the Old Testament revealed the Father clearly; the Gospels revealed the Son clearly; the life of the church (from Acts onward) revealed the Spirit clearly.

There's a pattern to God's self-revelation here, as each member of the Trinity comes clearly into focus at a different time.

The lateness of the full revelation of the Spirit, however, should in no way downplay the Spirit's divinity or importance. The Spirit is as much divine as the Father and the Son. We see clearly in Scripture that the Spirit is a person who performs divine actions (Luke 12:12), knows all the things God knows (1 Corinthians 2:10–11), does all the things that God does (Titus 3:5–6; Luke 1:67; Romans 5:3–5; Romans 15:16), and is equated with the Father and the Son in saving us through baptism (Matthew 28:19).

In all these things Scripture shows that the Spirit is coequal with the Father and the Son in the entire work of creating and redeeming us.

As Paul says in Ephesians 3:16–17, it is *by* the Spirit that the Father allows Jesus to live in us: "I pray that out of his glorious riches he may strengthen you with power through his Spirit in your inner being, so that Christ may dwell in your hearts through faith."

UNIT 6 / QUESTION 12:
WHAT DOES THE HOLY SPIRIT DO?

 It is important to continually remember that God enabling our ability to repent is not the same thing as God making us repent. Grace empowers our free wills.

Without God's work through the Spirit we would be unable to turn toward Him. But with God's help we have the choice.

Thomas Oden, a systematic theologian, said it this way:

> The Spirit does not coerce or overleap or overpower human self-determination, but persuades, coaxes, challenges, pries loose, and invites freedom. . . . If it were strictly a matter of the Spirit coercing the human will, then there could be no call to any duty of repentance, as there is in Scripture: "Repent, then, and turn to God, so that your sins may be wiped out, that times of refreshing may come from the Lord" (Acts 3:19). Such an appeal assumes that the hearer may or may not decide to repent. Enabled by grace, freedom is called to examine itself, its deceptions and evasions. God will not do the repenting for us (Thomas Oden, *Classic Christianity: A Systematic Theology*, 578).

Some theologians say the full range of gifts as described in New Testament (such as in passages like 1 Corinthians 12:1–11) are no longer available to us today. They say that these gifts (like speaking in tongues) were only for the early church. But there is good reason to believe that God still gives the full range of gifts even now. For one, there is much evidence of Christians practicing all the gifts. If we discounted all the accounts of healings or speaking in tongues then we would have to believe that millions of Christians are either liars or are self-deceived. This is a problem.

Furthermore, there is no strong evidence in Scripture that indicates these gifts will cease. And many church fathers who lived after the time of Jesus and the apostles record miraculous works like healings.

Christians should not write off the gifts of the Spirit too quickly. It is true that they seem to be more present in different places and times. But this fits perfectly with the way that the gifts of the Spirit's work are described in the Bible. The Spirit is like a wind that "blows where it wills" (John 3:8), and the gifts of the Spirit are not distributed evenly, as Paul says, but given as the Spirit "determines" (1 Corinthians 12:11).

We cannot control when and if we will be given any extra gifts of the Spirit. But we can know this: if we need them, the Spirit will provide them.

UNIT 7 / QUESTION 13: WHAT IS THE CHURCH?

The word for church in Greek is *ekklesia*, which means "a gathering." It comes from the root words "called" and "out of." The church is the gathering together of people called by God out of the world. Understanding the meaning of the word helps us to focus on the nature of the church as a special community—different from the world and called for a purpose.

One of the defining features of the life of the church is the unity in love that we have for one another (John 13:35). And not only unity with other Christians in our local church, but Christians everywhere, throughout time and space.

In the words of the Nicene Creed, the church is described as "one, holy, catholic, and apostolic." Two of the terms used to describe the church—"one" and "catholic"—touch on the importance of Christian unity. The church is called, again and again, to be "one" by the writers of the New Testament. For instance, Paul wrote in Romans 12:5, "so in Christ we, though many, form one body, and each member belongs to all the others."

And the church is catholic (which means, in this sense, "universal") because it is composed of all true believers everywhere. Christians are united with other believers around the world, be they Roman Catholic, Eastern Orthodox, Baptist, Methodist, or Pentecostal. We should be wary of dismissing the faith of other Christians who share the same essential creed, keeping in mind Jesus' words in John 10:16: "I have other sheep that are not of this sheep pen. I must bring them also. They too will listen to my voice, and there shall be one flock and one shepherd." Jesus is the shepherd of all Christians who obey His voice, even those whose churches look different than ours, but whose faith is the same in all essential matters.

A third-century bishop, Cyprian of Carthage, used the images of the sun and a tree to capture the ways that the church can spread out across the world, and have much diversity, while still remaining one:

> The Church is one, and by her fertility she has extended by degree into many. In the same way, the sun has many rays, but a single light; a tree has many branches but a single trunk resting on a deep root. (Cited in Alister McGrath, *The Christian Theology Reader*, 4th ed., 409)

This unity that we have with all believing Christians, however, is not just across space, but is also across time. The church is not just trying to be unified with other Christians living now but with all Christians from the time of the apostles. This is why the Nicene Creed also includes "apostolic," alongside "one, holy, [and] catholic."

To be "apostolic" means to be faithful to the church's essential teaching as it has been understood from the beginning. We aren't free to create a new idea of what it means to be Christian, even if everyone around us agrees. We realize that our faith has been passed on to us by those who came before. The essentials of the Christian faith have been preserved by those dead saints who have protected it, and who are still part of the church in a very real sense. We are surrounded, as Hebrews 12:1 says it, by a "great cloud of witnesses." Faithful people from the past who received the good news and handed it down to us. This is literally what tradition means, to "hand down."

Now, this does not mean that the church is utterly reliant in everything on tradition. God works in the world in all kinds of unexpected ways. He calls out new sheep to be part of His flock in ways that surprise us. For this reason, we must keep in mind that the animating life of the church is the activity of the Spirit, enabling us to be Christ's body in the world. Wherever the Spirit is at work, gathering those called by God to faithfully follow Jesus, following the teaching of the apostles, there is the church.

In talking about the different kinds of people in the church, I haven't gone very deeply into all the ways that our difference is a great strength. But this is an important theme in the Bible. It is not just that our differences create challenges to be overcome, but also that our differences complement each other as well.

For instance, in Ephesians 4:11–13, Paul talked about the way that God has given the church all kinds of different leaders to help it fully carry out Jesus' mission:

> So Christ himself gave the apostles, the prophets, the evangelists, the pastors and teachers, to equip his people for works of service, so that the body of Christ may be built up until we all reach unity in the faith and in the knowledge of the Son of God and become mature, attaining to the whole measure of the fullness of Christ.

Apostles, prophets, evangelists, pastors, and teachers are different kinds of calling, tailored to different kinds of people. Paul, an apostle, relied on pastors to stay behind and tend to the churches he had begun. Without pastors, the work of the apostles would be in vain. These different kinds of calling work together to help the church to be well-rounded (or "mature").

Probably in your church, there are people who gravitate toward different kinds of ministry. Apostles like to get new programs up and going, but then need helpers to keep them running. Teachers like to teach classic truths to the next generation of Christians in Sunday school, while prophetic types will focus on hearing fresh words from God through prayer. Evangelists will delight in preaching on Sundays, while pastor types will look forward to visiting the sick in hospitals.

All of these types are needed because all of us need something they bring to the whole body. None of us can only be one, isolated part of the body. We need each person in the church to help understand fully what it means to follow Jesus.

UNIT 7 / QUESTION 14:
WHAT ARE THE CHURCH'S SACRAMENTS?

1. Dallas Willard, *The Divine Conspiracy* (New York, NY: HarperCollins, 2009), 302.

2. There are many ways that God gives us grace: through reading the Bible, preaching, prayer, and many other means. But by "sacrament," Protestants mean a specially commanded action that was instituted by Jesus, which narrows the list down to two actions: *baptism* and *communion*.

The sacraments of baptism and communion have an outward sign (the water; the bread and wine), and also provide an invisible grace. It is necessary to keep the physical and the invisible aspects of the sacraments in mind. God, in His wisdom, has brought together the physical and the spiritual through these actions. (Much in the same way, He brought the physical and the spiritual together in the God-man Jesus Christ.) We are physical beings, so God gives us tangible things to do as Christians. And we are spiritual beings, so God graciously uses our physical actions to give us divine grace through them.

One error that Christians sometimes fall into is to think of the sacraments as mere reminders of deeper spiritual realities. Baptism or communion, in this sense, is just a mere "symbol." It is a symbol, but not *only* that. It is a symbol that also *does* something. In this way it's like a dollar bill, which is an image on paper, but also has a special power to do things in the real world (like buy a pack of gum).

It is also important to keep in mind that the sacraments are not *magic*. The actions themselves do not give us grace. It is God, *using* these actions, that gives them their power. Martin Luther wrote of baptism (though it applies to communion as well):

> Hence we ought to receive baptism from the hand of man just as if Christ Himself, nay, God Himself, were baptizing us with His own hands. For it is not a man's baptism, but that of Christ and God; though we receive it by the hand of a man. Even so any other creature which we enjoy through

the hand of another is really only God's. Beware then of making any such distinction in baptism, as to attribute the outward rite to man, and the inward blessing to God. Attribute both of them to God alone, and consider the person of him who confers baptism in no other light than as the vicarious instrument of God. (Martin Luther, "The Babylonian Captivity of the Church")

Perhaps the best Old Testament analogy to the sacrament of baptism is circumcision. Through circumcision, one was marked as a member of God's covenant people (see Genesis 17). And this was a one-time symbolic action that represented a deeper commitment to God. Baptism, too, is a once-and-for-all action by which we join the church. Even if we fall away from following Jesus for a time, we do not need to be re-baptized.

Also, like circumcision, baptism is often done to those who have not yet had personal faith. Rather, infants are being initiated into the household of God by their faithful parents, so that the child can grow in grace as a full member of the church. In this sense, baptism is like a gift that is given before we are even fully aware of its effects (this is true even for adults).

What baptism does (even infant baptism) is provide grace to us to wash us of sin and empower us for holiness. But it should be kept in mind that repentance and justifying faith are still needed to save us.

All grace is somewhat mysterious, and the sacraments are no exception. In fact, the Greek word for sacrament is "mystery" (*musterion*). We can say this much: in infant baptism, the grace that is given is like the grace given to us in salvation. It has many of the same effects, but it is still a particular kind of "prevenient grace" (to use Wesley's term discussed in the notes of Question 4). It is a grace that prepares children to respond to God's call to repent and believe (cf. Thomas Oden, *Classic Christianity*, 628–29).

Martin Luther wrote that "the baptism of infants is pleasing to Christ is sufficiently proved from His own work, namely, that God sanctifies many of them who have been thus baptized, and has given them the Holy Ghost" (*Larger Catechism*, "Of Infant Baptism").

Though the question of infant baptism is a sore issue in the church, with many denominations refusing to practice it, it should not be a matter that ultimately divides us. For one, it has been practiced very far back in the Christian tradition. The practice of believer's baptism is, in the larger timescale of the church, a relatively new thing. As Luther pointed out,

> If God did not accept the baptism of infants . . . during this long time unto this day no man upon earth could have been a Christian. Now, since God confirms Baptism by the gifts of His Holy Ghost, as is plainly perceptible in some of the church fathers, as St. Bernard, Gerson, John Hus, and others, who were baptized in infancy, and since the holy Christian Church cannot perish until the end of the world, they must acknowledge that such infant baptism is pleasing to God. (Ibid.)

It is a common saying that "we are what we eat." This is often taken to mean that if we eat healthily, we'll be healthy. And vice versa. The story of the Bible affirms this, but in a different way. In Scripture, what we eat is also given great importance. In the Old Testament, faithful Jews were forbidden to eat like their surrounding neighbors, to keep them set apart. In the New Testament, the old food laws were taken away. All foods were then pronounced clean, a symbol of the opening up of God's family to all the nations (Acts 10:9–16).

The theme of food is most clearly seen in Genesis 2:15–17, when humans were given every good tree to eat of, and prohibited from only one tree. Then, we defined ourselves by eating the wrong thing. In other words, by being hungry for sin. We became what we ate.

It should be no surprise then that Jesus makes eating the central act of Christian worship. The church's weekly celebration of communion intends to reverse the pattern of the fall by making us hungry for God. In eating the bread and wine, which become for us the body and blood, we become what we eat. We become like Jesus Christ. (For more on this, read Alexander Schmemann's *For the Life of the World*.)

Again, the reason that communion has this power is not simply because it reminds us of Jesus' death, but because it is, as John Wesley often put it, a "means of grace."

The only way that we can maintain our lives in Christ is by God's grace, and communion is a specially given way to transmit grace to us. In this sense, it is like medicine for our souls.

Communion is also the greatest sign of the church's unity. It is our family meal together as God's children. In lesson of Question 5, I talked about the way that the covenants worked in the Old Testament. Through a particular sign, God made a promise that created a people. (For instance, through the law given to Moses, God promised to be the God of Israel, a holy nation.) In the New Testament, Jesus called the cup of communion the "new covenant" (Luke 22:20).

The sacrament of communion is the sign of the new covenant. It is the visible sign of the new promise made by God in Christ that creates a new people. As we gather around the table, we show ourselves to be God's family.

UNIT 8 / QUESTION 15:
WHAT IS THE WORLD'S GREAT HOPE?

The analogy of the story of Scripture as a five-act play is spelled out more clearly in N. T. Wright's "How Can the Bible Be Authoritative?" (*Vox Evangelica* 21 [1991]: 7–32). It is also discussed, at length, in Craig Bartholomew and Michael Goheen's book *The Drama of Scripture.*

A key idea for Wright, Bartholomew, and Goheen is that knowing our place in the play helps us know how we are to *act* as Christians before the end of the story.

A key word Bartholomew and Goheen use is "improvisation." Sometimes actors in a play have to improvise lines (perhaps because another character forgot theirs and the next scripted line won't fit). When we improvise, we have to draw on what we know about the story and the character we are playing to come up with new creative lines that fit.

N. T. Wright gives this example,

Suppose there exists a Shakespeare play whose fifth act had been lost. The first four acts provide, let us suppose, such a wealth of characterization, such a crescendo of excitement within the plot, that it is generally agreed that the play ought to be staged. Nevertheless, it is felt inappropriate actually to write a fifth act once and for all: it would freeze the play into one form, and commit Shakespeare as it were to being prospectively responsible for work not in fact his own. Better, it might be felt, to give the key parts to highly trained, sensitive and experienced Shakespearean actors, who would immerse themselves in the first four acts, and in the language and culture of Shakespeare and his time, *and who would then be told to work out a fifth act for themselves* ("How Can the Bible Be Authoritative?" *Vox Evangelica* [1991] 21, 7–32).

In this case the actors are not free to radically rewrite the play. They have to be faithful to the first four acts. Therefore, to faithfully perform the role they have been given requires a certain measure of creativity.

Our situation as Christians, here and now, is kind of like that. We know the story that has come before us. And we know how the story will end. Our role is to continue playing out the story of Scripture faithfully, but also creatively. We might call this "faithful improvisation" (or as Bartholomew and Goheen call it "innovation [with] consistency") (*The Drama of Scripture* [Grand Rapids, MI: Baker Academic, 2004], 200).

This period of faithful improvisation is the story of the early church till now. The early church faced issues that Jesus did not address directly (such as whether Gentile Christians should be circumcised), and had to figure out how to respond in the moment while still being true to the gospel. Today we face challenges the early church didn't and so must come up with innovative answers that will fit with the story that came before and the end that is coming.

Sometimes our creative responses will be *joyful and unexpected*, anticipating the happy ending. Often they will be *painful and costly*, steering us to the cross and creating tragedy for the moment. But they must always be *faithful*. And so long as they are faithful, God has promised us that He can work all of our choices into a beautifully happy ending (Romans 8:28).

2 Very often, the best part in a book is after the climax but before the very end. J. R. R. Tolkien's *The Lord of the Rings* has a beautiful chapter called "The Scouring of the Shire," in which the heroic hobbits return to their homes, and set to right all the things that have gone wrong in their absence. Having been battle-hardened by their journey, they are capable of restoring the Shire to its former beauty and even making it better. Sam brings soil from the Elves, and sows it, bringing about a huge crop for years to come.

The period of the church, from the book of Acts till now, is like that. Emboldened by the victory of Jesus in Jerusalem, the church spreads to all the corners of the earth to spread the good news and bring redemption (Acts 1:8).

3 The Bible tells us that we will be fully redeemed to be like Jesus in the resurrection. But it also tells us that all creation will be raised up into a new state of glory. Paul said in Romans 8:22–23 that the "whole creation groans" for this redemption. And all creation will be liberated from death in the end.

John Wesley, in his sermon, "The General Deliverance," wrote that the whole of creation (animals included),

> will then, undoubtedly, be restored, not only to the vigour, strength, and swiftness which they had at their creation, but to a far higher degree of each than they ever enjoyed . . . [T]hey will suffer no more, either from within or without; the days of their groaning are ended. At the same time, there can be no reasonable doubt, but all the horridness of their appearance, and all the deformity of their aspect, will vanish away, and be exchanged for their primeval beauty. And with their beauty their happiness will return; to which there can then be no obstruction. As there will be nothing within, so there will be nothing without, to give them any uneasiness: no heat or cold, no storm or tempest, but one perennial spring. In the new earth, as well as in the new heavens, there will be nothing to give pain, but everything that the wisdom and goodness of God can create to give happiness. As a recompense for what they once suffered, while under the "bondage of corruption," when God has "renewed the face of the earth," and their corruptible body has put on incorruption, they shall

enjoy happiness suited to their state, without alloy, without interruption, and without end.

For anyone who loves, not just God and humans, but also animals and the rest of creation, this is very good news—for us and for them. It means that all the best of created life will not be ended with Christ's return. It will be *perfected*.

One important truth to keep in mind is that the phrase "the kingdom of heaven," especially when used by Jesus in the book of Matthew, does not refer to a place "up" where God is and where we will go as well. "Heaven" refers to any place where God rules. And Jesus' mission is not to bring us up to heaven but to bring heaven down to earth.

N. T. Wright, in his book, *The Lord & His Prayer*, pointed out that the final promise of redemption pictured at the end of the book of Revelation is given in Jesus' words in the Lord's Prayer. We do not pray to go *to* God's kingdom (or "heaven"), but for God to bring His kingdom "down":

> "Heaven" and "earth" are the two interlocking arenas of God's good world. Heaven is God's space, where God's writ runs and God's future purposes are waiting in the wings. Earth is our world, our space. Think of the vision at the end of Revelation. It isn't about humans being snatched up *from* earth to heaven. The holy city, new Jerusalem, comes down from heaven to earth. God's space and ours are finally married, integrated at last. That is what we pray for when we pray "thy Kingdom come." (*The Lord & His Prayer* [Grand Rapids, MI: Eerdmans, 1997], 24–25)

Wright's use of marriage language is not accidental. The end of the book of Revelation shows us the heavenly city, the new Jerusalem, *descending* to the earth "prepared as a bride beautifully dressed for her husband" (21:1–2).

In the end, heaven and earth will be finally united.

Jesus descends, then ascends again. But when He returns He brings heaven down with Him.

This is something that has not happened fully yet, but it does happen partially now. When we faithfully follow Jesus, we help God's kingdom to "come" down to earth, anticipating the final, ultimate marriage of heaven and earth.

UNIT 8 / QUESTION 16:
WHAT IS OUR FUTURE?

This misconception is very common in the church. Many people forget that after we die we won't be disembodied spirits, but have fully resurrected, healthy bodies. If anything, we should expect that after the resurrection the pleasures of our bodily life will *increase*, not *diminish*.

It is true that sometimes the ways that Scripture describes eternal life don't appeal to us naturally. For instance, the eternal praising of God in heaven, as described in the book of Revelation, might make us worry that heaven will be boring. But this is not a problem with Scripture as much as it is a problem with us.

We think that being in God's presence, forever, will get boring because we can't really imagine the perfection of God. But at the very least, we can understand in theory that if something is perfect, we'll never get tired of it. We get tired of things down here because they aren't perfect.

In the Bible, God uses images that try and help us imagine enjoying *infinite* perfection by using some of the best *finite* things we know about.

C. S. Lewis has some biting words to say on this topic. He wrote:

> There is no need to be worried by facetious people who try to make the Christian hope of "Heaven" ridiculous by saying they do not want "to spend eternity playing harps." The answer to such people is that if they cannot understand books written for grown-ups, they should not talk about them. All the scriptural imagery (harps, crowns, gold, etc.) is, of course, a merely symbolical attempt to express the inexpressible. Musical instruments are mentioned because for many people (not all) music is the thing known in the present life which most strongly suggests ecstasy and

infinity. Crowns are mentioned to suggest the fact that those who are united with God in eternity share His splendour and power and joy. Gold is mentioned to suggest the timelessness of Heaven (gold does not rust) and the preciousness of it. People who take these symbols literally might as well think that when Christ told us to be like doves, He meant that we were to lay eggs (C. S. Lewis, *Mere Christianity*, 137).

2. An ancient theologian named Methodius of Olympus compared the resurrected body to a beautiful, metal statue that had been damaged by a jealous person who hated its beauty. Seeing the way his creation had been defaced, the original sculpture wanted to set it right. But the damage to the statue was so great that it had to be melted down and recast so that it would be perfect again.

Methodius compares the melting and recasting of the statue with our own death and resurrection in glory. He wrote,

> Now it seems to me that God's plan was much the same as this human example. He saw that humanity, his most wondrous creation, has been corrupted by envy and treachery. Such was his love for humanity that he could not allow it to continue in this condition, remaining faulty and deficient to eternity. For this reason, God dissolved humanity once more into the original materials, so that it could be remodeled in such a way that all its defects could be eliminated and disappear. Now the melting down of a statue corresponds to the death and dissolution of the human body, and the remoulding of the material to the resurrection after death. (Cited by Alister McGrath, *The Christian Theology* Reader, Fourth ed., 541)

This is a good analogy, because it captures the way the full image of God, which was destroyed in the fall, is recreated in the resurrection. The analogy is incomplete because glorified, resurrected humans will surpass the original creation. We'll be immortal, perfected in knowledge, and protected from future sin. In this sense, the recast statue of glorified humanity is like the original, but even more beautiful.

3. In one sense, misery is simply the natural result of rejecting God. As Augustine said, "You have made us for yourself, O Lord, and our hearts are restless until they find their rest in you" (*Confessions*, 1.1).

Like a single puzzle piece, we are made to fit into God's larger picture to be complete. In rejecting God we're rejecting our ultimate purpose—the thing we were designed for: loving relationship.

Trying to be happy without God is like trying to be full without food. It doesn't work.

One of the most terrifying thoughts we can ever conceive is the idea of eternal hell. The very thought of damnation is enough to send shudders down the spine of almost anyone.

The utter terror of hell has led some to deny that a good God would allow anyone to go there. Surely, many may think, *if God is perfectly just, He would not allow people to go to hell simply for not believing in Him.*

The decision of God to condemn some people to hell might seem to be unfair, or even arbitrary. For instance, Jesus said in Matthew 7:22–23 that on the day of judgment, "Many will say to me on that day, 'Lord, Lord, did we not prophesy in your name and in your name drive out demons and in your name perform many miracles?'" We then hear what Jesus will say: "I never knew you. Away from me, you evildoers!"

Here we might object, thinking that Jesus is unfairly condemning many who tried to do their best.

One thing to consider in this verse is that those who say these things to Jesus on the last day are still trying to justify themselves by their actions. But we know that our actions are never good enough to pay the debt. These people want to get into the kingdom of heaven based on what *they* have done, not based on what Jesus has done.

Another thing is to hear in those words the lovelessness of those Jesus sends away. And this is important. Because, as we've talked about already, salvation requires that we believe in God, which means more than believing *that* God exists. It means trusting in Him. It means we have a relationship with God. In other words, we *love* God and do all good works as a desire to please Him. Even in this imaginary conversation Jesus offers to us, there is an important clue to why people go to hell: they do not love God nor desire to be with Him.

In this sense, damnation is simply the natural result of rejecting God's loving invitation. Even if God let unbelievers into His eternal kingdom, they wouldn't be happy, because they don't want to be in loving relationship with God.

Now, it is also important to keep in mind that the church, as one body, has not defined a specific doctrine of damnation, so there is some liberty to believe different things about what damnation looks like. But the strong words of Jesus about hell demand that we take it as reality (Matthew 25:46).

Yet this is also true: because of what we know about the character of God, we can have assurance that God is working to save all the people that He can. First Timothy 2:4 says God wants "all people to be saved."

God's justice demands punishment for sin. But God's love is the underlying motive behind everything He does. It is because of God's love, in fact, that there is a hell. Because God loves us so much, He gives us the ability to respond freely to His call. In the end, only those who reject God's love will ever have to bear the punishment of His justice.

For more teaching resources that go with this book, please visit
seedbed.com/absolutebasics

CPSIA information can be obtained
at www.ICGtesting.com
Printed in the USA
LVHW030916151222
735051LV00003B/3